BOOKKEEPING

The Ultimate Guide For Beginners to Learn in Step by Step The Simple and Effective Methods of Bookkeeping for Small Business with proven Tips to Succeed In Bookkeeping

MAX RUELL

Text Copyright © Max Ruell

All rights reserved. No part of this guide may be reproduced in any form without permission in writing from the publisher except in the case of brief quotations embodied in critical articles or reviews.

Legal & Disclaimer

The information contained in this book and its contents is not designed to replace or take the place of any form of medical or professional advice; and is not meant to replace the need for independent medical, financial, legal or other professional advice or services, as may be required. The content and information in this book have been provided for educational and entertainment purposes only.

The content and information contained in this book has been compiled from sources deemed reliable, and it is accurate to the best of the Author's knowledge, information and belief. However, the Author cannot guarantee its accuracy and validity and cannot be held liable for any errors and/or omissions. Further, changes are periodically made to this book as and when needed. Where appropriate and/or necessary, you must consult a professional (including but not limited to your doctor, attorney, financial advisor or such other professional advisor) before using any of the suggested remedies, techniques, or information in this book.

Upon using the contents and information contained in this book, you agree to hold harmless the Author from and against any damages, costs, and expenses, including any legal fees potentially resulting from the application of any of the information provided by this book. This disclaimer applies to any loss, damages or injury caused by the use and application, whether directly or indirectly, of any advice or information presented, whether for breach of contract, tort, negligence, personal injury, criminal intent, or under any other cause of action.

You agree to accept all risks of using the information presented inside this book.

You agree that by continuing to read this book, where appropriate and/or necessary, you shall consult a professional (including but not limited to your doctor, attorney, or financial advisor or such other advisor as needed) before using any of the suggested remedies, techniques, or information in this book.

Table of Contents

Introduction 1

Chapter 1: **What Is Bookkeeping?**......................................4

How Bookkeeping Works..4
Why Bookkeeping?..5

Chapter 2: **Accounting System** 7

Definition Of Important Accounting Terms 7
Choosing Your Accounting System 11
Cash Versus Accrual-Based Accounting 12
Cash-Based Accounting..12
Benefits Of Cash-Based Accounting.................................12
Downsides Of Cash-Based Accounting............................13
Which Types Of Businesses Can Use Cash-Based Accounting System?..13
Accrual-Based Accounting..14

Chapter 3: **Choosing Your Accounting System** 16

Single-Entry Versus Double-Entry Bookkeeping..........16
Single-Entry Bookkeeping 16
Advantages Of Single-Entry Bookkeeping System..........17
Disadvantages Of Single-Entry Bookkeeping System.....17
Which Businesses Can Use Single-Entry Bookkeeping System 18
Double-Entry Bookkeeping...18
Reason For Double-Entry Bookkeeping And The Benefits 18
Downsides Of The Double-Entry Bookkeeping System...19

Which Businesses Can Use Double-Entry Bookkeeping System? 19
Cash Versus Accrual-Based Accounting 19
Cash Based Accounting 20
Benefits Of Cash Based Accounting 20
Downsides Of Cash Based Accounting 20
Which Types Of Businesses Can Use Cash Based Accounting System? 21
Accrual Based Accounting 22
Benefits Of Accrual Based Accounting System 23
Downsides Of Accrual Based Accounting System 23
Which Types Of Businesses Should Use Accrual Based Accounting System? 24

Chapter 4: How To Set Up A Single-Entry Bookkeeping System For Your Business 25

Set Up Your Cashbook 25
The Columns Of The Cashbook 26
Cashbook Example 27
Create Your Profit And Loss Statement 28
Create Your Balance Sheet 29
Set Up Your Bank Reconciliation Statement 30

Chapter 5: How To Set Up A Double-Entry Bookkeeping System For Your Business 32

Assets 32
Liabilities 33
Equity 34
Create Chart Of Accounts 34
Start With The Source Documents 35
Post Transactions In Your Journals 36
Cash Account [Asset Account] 37
Bank Account [Asset Account] 38

 Accounts Payable Journal [Liability Account]................ 38
 Stationery Account [Expenses Account]....................... 39
 Accounts Payable [Liability Account]............................ 39
 Sales Journal 40
 Bank Account [Asset Account] 42
Transfer Your Journal Entries To Your General Ledger 43
 Bank Account [Asset Account] 44
Create Your Trial Balance... 45
Create Your Profit And Loss Accounts/Income Statement 47
Prepare Your Balance Sheet 50

Chapter 6: **The Balance Sheet** 51

How Can I Use This Financial Document? 51
The Balance Sheet For The Securities And Exchange Commission.. 53
What Are The Different Types Of Assets? 56
 Current Assets... 56
 Non-Current Assets 57
What Are The Different Liabilities? 58
Shareholders' Equity 59

Chapter 7: **The Cash Flow Statement** 60

The Structure Of Your Cash Flow Statement.................. 61
Operating Activities 62
How Can I Calculate My Cash Flow? 64
The Investing Activities And Your Cash Flow Statement 67
Financing Activities And Your Cash Flow Statement .. 68
Tying Together The Income Statement, The Balance Sheet, And The Cash Flow Statement.............................. 69

Chapter 8: **Tax Accounting** 72

iii

What Is Tax Accounting? 73
The Tax Principles Vs. GAAP 74
Tax Accounting And How It Works For An Individual
.... 75
Tax Accounting For A Business 76
How Tax Accounting Works For Organizations Exempt
From Taxes 77

Chapter 9: **The Cost Principle** 79

The Issue With The Cost Principle 80
Is The Cost Principle Applied At All Times? 81

Chapter 10: **Alternatives To GAAP And Everything They Imply** 83

Are Alternative GAAP Methods Misleading? 84
How To Disclose Non-GAAP Measures 87
Contemporary Debate Against Non-GAAP 90
How Common Accounting Concepts Connect To GAAP
And Alternatives To GAAP 92
Revenue Recognition 92
Uncollectible Accounts 95
Inventories 96
Depreciable Assets 97
Leases 99
Understanding How The Standards Are Set 101
How Are The Alternatives To GAAP Used? 106
Other Comprehensive Basis Of Accounting 108
What Is Considered OCBOA? 110

Chapter 11: **Why Your Business Needs Quickbooks** .. 113

Reasons For Maintaining An Accounting System 113
What Quickbooks Does 115
Reasons For Using Quickbooks 116

Chapter 12: **What Is Quickbooks?**..................................**119**

Brief Background 120
Factors To Consider For Quickbooks First-Timers 121

Chapter 13: **Quickbooks Versions For Small Businesses** **123**

Which Quickbooks Version Should You Buy? 124
Does Your Business Use Macs? 124
Does Your Business Handle A Lot Of General Accounting Functions? 124
Do You Run Your Business On-The-Go Or Remotely? 125
Do You Need A Version That Is Specific To Your Industry? 125
Does Your Business Need To Track Inventory For Both Raw Materials And Finished Products? 125
Quickbooks Pro Edition..126
Quickbooks Enterprise..127
Quickbooks Online Edition 128
Quickbooks For Mac 131
Quickbooks Premier 133

Chapter 14: **Quickbooks Online**..**135**

Quickbooks Online 135
The Cloud Benefits Of Quickbooks Online 136
This Is What You Get From Quickbooks Online 139
Quickbooks Desktop 139

Chapter 15: **Quickbooks For Inventory** **141**

Setting Up Quickbooks Inventory................................142
Prepare Your Lists 143
Types Of Items In The Items List..................................147

Chapter 16: **14 Tips And Tricks** **150**

Chapter 17: Mistakes To Avoid 161

Chapter 18: Definitions Of Bookkeeping Terms 165

Conclusion 172

Introduction

Whether you are just starting your business or have had your business for years, it is important to know bookkeeping.

Bookkeeping has been around for centuries. However, it has evolved over time to help your business keep track of your finances better.

Bookkeeping covers a long list of aspects that help the business owner make decisions about the company. To better understand bookkeeping, my goal is to help you get a good feel for knowing how to read the financial reports, the basics of bookkeeping, employees, understanding the balance sheet and income statement, and so much more.

Come along with me as we explore the world of bookkeeping and help you, the business owner, understand how to make sense out of bookkeeping.

As an added bonus, I have included a section for your business taxes. I also included a step-by-step process of preparing W-2 forms and the information that is needed for those. You will soon find out that there is more to it than just providing the information and typing it up on the W-2 form.

Keep reading, and you will see what it takes to get on the same page as your bookkeeper. I always said, "It is not the business owner that runs the business. It is the business owner teamed up with the bookkeeper that truly runs the business."

Running a business can be fun and rewarding. However, if you do not have the basic knowledge of the fundamental financial skills needed, it can prove to be stressful as well.

Throughout this book, you will learn the basics of bookkeeping and finding the right bookkeeper for you. As you go through it, you will also learn about the ledgers and journals. It is important that you know where your money is at all times. I also take the time to talk to you about hiring employees. Let's face it—if your business is going to grow above a certain level, you will eventually need to hire someone to work with you.

There is also a lot of software available to help you with all your bookkeeping needs, although not all accounting software is right for your business. We will take a look at a few of the top-rated applications and give you both the good and the bad of each one.

Don't forget: you also need to understand those scary financial statements. That's why we will take a look at the four main financial statements and break them down for you so that you can easily read and understand each one.

It does not matter if you have been in business for a couple of years or are just starting; you will be filing taxes at the end of the year. This is a lot of work, and your bookkeeper can help you get prepared.

Did you know that as a business owner, you can deduct a lot of your expenses? I included that as well. It is only a small list, and with a little research, you could probably find more.

Finally, I also included, in detail, how to go about preparing, distributing, and filing the employees' W-2s.

So, come along with me as we take this glorious adventure into bookkeeping for small businesses and give you the power to understand your business's financial health.

Chapter 1:

What Is Bookkeeping?

Simply put, bookkeeping is the process of recording a business's financial transactions, such as its sales, purchases, payments, and receipts, on a daily basis.

These records must be accurate and up-to-date and should be able to provide a clear picture of the performance of the business after a specific period.

How Bookkeeping Works

Whenever any individual or corporate body buys anything from you or sells anything to you, you have to record the exact details of the transaction and keep the documents used to transact the business as backup evidence.

You would then use the individual records you have made to set up financial statements at the end of a period, which could be daily, weekly, monthly, or yearly.

Why Bookkeeping?

Bookkeeping may involve historical records, but these records are very vital to the success of any business.

Here are some of the very important reasons for bookkeeping:

- Bookkeeping provides a true and accurate picture of the business. To know how your business is performing, whether you are making gains or losses, growing or dwindling, the only way you can know these is if you keep accurate records.

- There is the issue of taxes; you have to be able to know just how much taxes you need to pay at the end of every year.

- It helps you easily forecast and create plans for your business. By looking at your bookkeeping records, you can easily say, "We always sell 500 units of X product every December, so this year, we should work on increasing our sales to XX units."

- If you have investors or third parties such as shareholders or partners who would be interested in the performance of your business, well-kept books are the only way you can show them how your business is really doing.

- Through bookkeeping, you can also easily figure out thefts, dishonesty, or poor performances if you have employees or people running your business for you.

- Another benefit you can derive from adequate business bookkeeping is that you can use your financial statements as proofs of business performance if you need to secure loans for your business.

- Bookkeeping shall also help you monitor your business expenses in relation to income.

With that understanding on the importance of bookkeeping, let's now move on to understanding some key terms that are used in bookkeeping and accounting in general before we can get to the point of discussing how to go about bookkeeping.

Chapter 2:

Accounting System

Definition of Important Accounting Terms

To understand bookkeeping, you need to understand some very important accounting terms, most of which we will cover below:

Assets: Your assets are any resources or things of value owned by your business whose utility is not limited to a single accounting period and whose value can be reasonably estimated.

An example of an asset is a building; the building is relevant to your business for more than one year, and you can easily estimate the financial value of the building. On the other hand, your electricity bill for last month does not count as an asset because the value is only limited to a specific period.

Assets can be tangible like buildings and equipment, or intangible things like intellectual properties and trademarks.

Equity: Equity refers to the ownership interest (stock or contributions) in a business or in a personal asset. For instance, if your home is worth $200,000 and you still have a mortgage loan of $80,000, it means you have $120,000 equity on the house, or if you and your partner each contribute $50,000 to start a business worth $100,000, it means you both have 50% equity in the business.

Liability: Liabilities refer to your business obligations. You can also see it as what your business owes to other people. It could be money you borrowed, responsibilities you owe to others, or a transaction that has already occurred but is yet to be paid for.

Debit (dr.) and credit (cr.): In accounting, credit is anything that reduces your assets or expenses account or increases your liability or equity account.

On the other hand, debit is any transaction that decreases your liability or equity account or increases your assets or expenses account.

In double entry bookkeeping (more on that later), every transaction affects two accounts; one account gains something while the other account loses something. The account that loses value is credited while the one that gains value is debited.

Below is an example of the use of debit and credit in accounting:

Your business, XYZ Limited buys equipment for $10,000 on credit. This means that your equipment and machinery (assets) has an addition to it, so you debit that account. Nevertheless, since you have not paid for the equipment, you are still indebted. This means your business liability account has increased so what you would do is to credit your accounts payable (liability) account to reflect this increase.

See the illustration below:

Debit

Credit

Equipment and machinery account (fixed assets)

$10,000

Accounts payable

$10,000

Let's take another example category. Assuming XYZ Ltd. sells a product to a customer for $500; it means that the business earns revenue of $500 and that there is an increase in cash (assets) of $500, so you debit the asset account and credit the revenue account.

Debit

Credit

Cash

$500

Revenue

$500

We shall deeply discuss debits and credits in section 3. In the meantime, here is a basic rule for crediting and debiting accounts.

- Increase in asset–debit
- Increase in expenses–debit
- Decrease in liability (when you finally make payments from money you owe)–debit
- Decrease in equity–debit
- Increase in liability (when you incur fresh debts or add to the existing ones)–credit
- Increase in equity–credit
- Decrease in assets–credit
- Decrease in expenses–credit

Revenue/income: In accounting, revenue and income often have interchangeable meaning and uses. Revenue refers to all monies earned by your business regardless of whether they have been collected at the time of reporting or otherwise.

Receipts: Receipts refer to the portion of revenue in business transactions already paid up.

Profits: In accounting, your profit refers to what remains of your revenue/income after you deducting all business expenses. Profits come in two categories: net profits and gross profits.

Gross profits equal your total sales less the costs of goods sold (such as the cost of raw materials, production, delivery costs, etc.) while net profit equals your gross profit less other business expenses not directly related to sales of goods such as taxes, costs of depreciation, and interests.

Losses: Losses refer to any reduction in net income or assets of your business.

With that understanding of the basic terms, let's now learn about some basic principles of accounting.

Choosing Your Accounting System

When choosing your accounting system, you need to make two major decisions:

1. Cash versus accrual-based accounting
2. Double-entry versus single-entry bookkeeping

Cash versus Accrual-Based Accounting

There are two different methods used to record accounting transactions: the cash-based method and the accrual-based method. Choose the most suitable one for your business depending on the size of the business.

Cash-Based Accounting

Under this accounting system, you only record revenue/income and expenses whenever there is an actual exchange of cash. You only record expenses and purchases when you have paid cash for them and income when a customer has paid for the goods/services.

For instance, if Mr. A buy a product or receives a service from you in January but does not pay for it until May, you would have to wait until May when Mr. A pay for it before you record the transactions.

Benefits of Cash-Based Accounting

Using the cash-based system of accounting has some advantages:

- Very simple and uncomplicated such that you can easily handle your bookkeeping with zero accounting knowledge/experience.

- You don't need complex software or accounting records; oftentimes, all you need is your check booklet.

Naturally, everything that has an upside also has a downside:

Downsides of Cash-Based Accounting

Cash-based accounting is not always advisable to use because it provides insufficient records and does not really provide a true and clear picture of what is really going on in the business. For instance, you could erroneously report that your business made losses in January because you were yet to receive payments for the products/services sold.

Cash-based accounting also focuses on revenues and expenses alone and ignores other aspects of the business such as assets, inventory, liabilities, equity, and so on.

It also does not conform to the generally accepted accounting principles (GAP) or international financial reporting standards (IFRS).

Which Types of Businesses can Use Cash-Based Accounting System?

Legally, only a few businesses have the green light to use the cash-based system of accounting. You can use cash-based accounting if your business falls within any of the following categories:

- Sole proprietorship with annual average gross receipts of less than $1,000,000

- S-Corporation with annual average gross receipts of less than $1,000,000

- C-Corporation with annual average gross receipts of less than $5,000,000

- A company not publicly traded or not under any obligation to make full disclosure to the IRS

- Family-owned farms with annual gross receipts of less than $25,000,000

Accrual-Based Accounting

Under the accrual-based accounting system, you record transactions when earnings are made and expenses are incurred, not when they are paid for.

In this case, dollar bills or checks do not have to exchange hands before you record such transactions; every time a transaction occurs, you have to record it in your books.

For example, let's assume YXL Ltd. hires you to repair some of its equipment in January and you charge them $5,000 for this service. However, YXL Ltd. does not issue a check immediately but promises to discuss it with the financial accountant and then get back to you. This system of accounting requires that you record this transaction in your accounts receivable books as soon as you complete the job whether YXL makes payments for it or not.

There are two major account items you have to record when using the accrual method of accounting:

Accounts receivable: Account receivable would include all the monies owed to your business not paid.

In this example, as soon as you send out your invoice for the sales of a product or service, you record the value in your account's receivable ledger.

This account helps you track everything owed to your business.

Accounts payable: Account payable is the exact opposite of accounts receivable. Here, you record all the monies your business owes to other people.

As soon as you receive an invoice or make a commitment to the other party, you have to record the transaction in your account payable book so you can track what your business owes to other people.

Chapter 3:

Choosing Your Accounting System

When choosing your accounting system, you need to make two major decisions:

1. Cash versus Accrual-Based Accounting
2. Double-Entry versus Single-Entry Bookkeeping

Single-Entry versus Double-Entry Bookkeeping

Another important decision you need to make for your business is whether you want to be using the single-entry bookkeeping system or the double entry bookkeeping method.

Single-Entry Bookkeeping

As the name implies, Single entry bookkeeping is a system of accounting where transactions are recorded just once as a single entry and not as debits and credits as is the case with the double entry bookkeeping system.

The single-entry bookkeeping system is very similar to the check register you use to track your deposits, payments, and balances for your checking account. This system of accounting does not require keeping any ledgers or journals; however, it is not compatible with the provisions of GAAP.

The next Section detailed discusses how to set up a single-entry bookkeeping system for your business.

Advantages of Single-Entry Bookkeeping System

The single-entry bookkeeping system is very simple and uncomplicated and you can easily set up and use this system even if you have very little accounting knowledge and experience.

When you use this system, you also get to save money because you do not need to hire an accountant to handle your financial or tax reports.

Disadvantages of Single-Entry Bookkeeping System

The single-entry system fails to provide sufficient records of your business and is thus not an ideal way to evaluate your company's true financial position or performance.

This type of account is also prone to lots of errors because there is no double-checking system in place.

Which Businesses Can Use Single-Entry Bookkeeping System

You can use the single-entry bookkeeping system if you are using the cash-based accounting system for your business.

Double-Entry Bookkeeping

Under the double-entry system of bookkeeping, every financial transaction affects two different accounts and therefore, has to be recorded twice i.e. a credit entry is made in one account, while an equal and corresponding debit entry is made in another account.

Reason for Double-Entry Bookkeeping and the Benefits

This method of accounting helps prevent errors in the accounts because it serves as an in-built error checking system.

At the end of each accounting period, the amount in the debit side of your account ledgers must be equal to the amounts on the credit side. If there is as much as a cent difference, it means that there is an error somewhere.

Downsides of the double-entry bookkeeping System

The major challenge with the double entry system of bookkeeping is that it is much more technical to set up and a lot more complex to understand but once you get a hang of the basics, you can manage it well.

Which Businesses can Use double-entry bookkeeping System?

Businesses that use the accrual-based system of accounting also need to use the double-entry system of bookkeeping.

Section 4 has more details about how to set up a double-entry bookkeeping system for your business.

Let's discuss how to set up a single-entry bookkeeping system if that's what you prefer to follow.

Cash versus Accrual-Based Accounting

There are two different methods used to record accounting transactions: the cash-based method and the accrual-based method. Choose the most suitable one for your business depending on the size of the business.

Cash Based Accounting

Under this accounting system, you only record revenue/income and expenses whenever there is an actual exchange of cash. You only record expenses and purchases when you have paid cash for them and income when a customer has paid for the goods/services.

For instance, if Mr. A buys a product or receives a service from you in January but does not pay for it until May, you would have to wait until May when Mr. A pays for it before you record the transactions.

Benefits of Cash Based Accounting

- Using the cash-based system of accounting has some advantages such as:
- Very simple and uncomplicated such that you can easily handle your bookkeeping with zero accounting knowledge/experience.
- You don't need complex software or accounting records; oftentimes, all you need is your check booklet.

Naturally, everything that has an upside also has a downside:

Downsides of Cash Based Accounting

Cash based accounting is not always advisable to use because it provides insufficient records and does not really provide a true and clear picture of what is really going on in the business. For instance, you could erroneously report that your business made losses in January because you were yet to receive payments for the products/services sold.

Cash based accounting also focuses on revenues and expenses alone and ignores other aspects of the business such as assets, inventory, liabilities, equity, and so on.

It also does not conform to the Generally Accepted Accounting Principles [GAP] or International Financial Reporting Standards [IFRS].

Which Types of Businesses can Use Cash Based Accounting System?

Legally, only a few businesses have the green light to use the cash-based system of accounting. You can use cash-based accounting if your business falls within any of the following categories:

- Sole proprietorship with annual average gross receipts of less than $1,000,000

- S-Corporation with annual average gross receipts of less than $1,000,000

- C-Corporation with annual average gross receipts of less than $5,000,000

- A company not publicly traded or not under any obligation to make full disclosure to the IRS

- Family-owned farms with annual gross receipts of less than $25,000,000.

Accrual Based Accounting

Under the accrual-based accounting system, you record transactions when earnings are made and expenses are incurred, not when they are paid for.

In this case, dollar bills or checks do not have to exchange hands before you record such transactions; every time a transaction occurs, you have to record it in your books.

For example, let's assume YXL Ltd. hires you to repair some of its equipment in January and you charge them $5,000 for this service. However, YXL Ltd. does not issue a check immediately but promises to discuss it with the financial accountant and then get back to you. This system of accounting requires that you record this transaction in your accounts receivable books as soon as you complete the job whether YXL makes payments for it or not.

There are two major account items you have to record when using the accrual method of accounting:

Accounts Receivable: Account receivable would include all the monies owed to your business not paid.

In this example, as soon as you send out your invoice for the sales of a product or service, you record the value in your accounts receivable ledger.

This account helps you track everything owed to your business.

Accounts Payable: Account payable is the exact opposite of accounts receivable. Here, you record all the monies your business owes to other people.

As soon as you receive an invoice or make a commitment to the other party, you have to record the transaction in your account payable book so you can track what your business owes to other people.

Benefits of Accrual Based Accounting System

Using the accrual-based system of accounting has many benefits.

- For starters, the accrual-based accounting system produces a more accurate and reliable accounting report, and gives a true and clear picture of the performance of the business.
- It also provides a basis for comparing your accounting results.

Downsides of Accrual Based Accounting System

This method of accounting is usually harder and more complicated than the cash-based method of accounting where you only need to record cash transactions.

Which types of Businesses Should Use Accrual Based Accounting System?

Use the accrual-based accounting system if your business is:

- A C-corporation
- Your business has inventory
- You are obligated by the IRS to make full disclosure of your business.
- Your business has gross sales revenue that is higher than $3million every year.

Chapter 4:

How to set up a Single-Entry Bookkeeping System for Your Business

As mentioned earlier, if your business is a small one or if your transactions are of very low volume, you can adopt a single-entry bookkeeping system for your business.

Essentially, you just need to keep a record of the income and expenses your business incurs using a cashbook and then generate a report from this at the end of the year. Here is how to go about it:

Set up Your Cashbook

A cashbook is a journal where you record all your business receipts and expenses. It usually has two columns, one column dedicated to recording all monies received by the business while the other column is used to record monies paid out by the business.

It covers for all expenses done in cash as well as those done through the bank.

At the end of a period, you use the cashbook to reconcile your bank statement and create your profit and loss statement as well as your balance sheet.

The Columns of the Cashbook

Your single-entry cashbook should have x columns as seen below:

Date: In this column, you can record the date of the transactions.

Description: Describe the nature of the transactions in details and put any other specific details that would help you differentiate each transaction from other similar ones.

Reference: You can include invoice numbers or create your own unique identification system that shall help you better identify each transaction.

Income: Here, you should insert the monetary value of all monies coming into the business.

Expenses: Insert the monetary value of all monies paid out of the business in this column.

Balance: This column reflects the money left within your business at each point in time. Every time money comes into your business, you add it to this balance and every time you spend money, you deduct it from this balance so that at a glance, you can always know just how much money remains within your business.

Cashbook Example

This is what your cashbook and the entries would look like:

Date	Description	Reference	Income	Expenses	Balance
1 November 2017	Starting balance for the week				$5,000
2 November 2017	Paid electricity bill for the month	ELC 002		[$200]	$4,800
5 November 2017	Purchase of Inventory	INV 007		[$3,000]	$1,800
6 November 2017	Rent	RNT 002		[$250]	$1,550
7 November 2017	Product Sales	SLS 001	$500		$2,050
7 November 2017	Sales Tax	SLT 003		[$43]	$2,007
8 November 2017	Bank Acct. Interest Received	INT 009	$120		$2,127
8 November 2017	Customer Refund Paid	RFN		[$50]	$2,077
8 November 2017	Ending Balance for the week				$2077

As you can see, we add all monies coming into the business to the balance, while we deduct from the balance all monies going out of the business. Your balance at the end of the week/month/year should be equal to the amount of money you have in your bank account or in your hands.

You can also add two extra columns for bank income and bank expenses if you plan to operate your business with cash and bank simultaneously.

Create Your Profit and Loss Statement

The next set of books you have to keep is your profit and loss statement. Also called the income statement, this helps you get a picture of what remains in your business as income after deducting all expenses.

What you have to do here is take all the values of your income, add it together, and then take all your expenses and add it together as well. Subtract your total income from your total expenses [do not add inventory since that is not a business income or expenses] and that gives you a figure for your profit or loss.

Using the example above, let us create your profit and loss statement for the week ended.

Profit and Loss Statement for the Week Ended 8th November, 2017			
	Expenses	**Income**	**Profit**
Electricity	$200		

Rent	$250		
Product Sales		$500	
Sales Tax	$43		
Bank Acct. Interest Received		$120	
Column Totals	$493	$620	
Profit [Income less Expenses]			$127

Create Your Balance Sheet

You cannot really create a standard balance sheet using a single-entry bookkeeping system. What you can create is a statement of affairs.

A statement of affairs helps show if there have been changes in the financial position of your business within a specified period. It can also ascertain if the business made profits during the period

Below is a format you can use to prepare a statement of affairs for your business.

	$
Closing Capital	XXXX
Less: Opening Capital	XXXX

Net Increase/Decrease	XXXX
Add drawings made during the period	XXXX
Less: Fresh Capital introduced during the period	XXXX
Less: Salary paid out to business owner	XXXX
Profit/Loss During the Year	XXXX

Your single-entry bookkeeping system essentially ends with the preparation of a statement of affairs for your business.

As you must have already seen, there is very little that the single-entry bookkeeping system can tell you and other people about your business. If you feel that this method is insufficient for your business, you can consider adopting the double-entry bookkeeping system as demonstrated in the next Section.

Set up Your Bank Reconciliation Statement

After the cashbook, the next step is to generate the bank reconciliation statement.

When you receive your bank statement at the end of the period, the balance you have on it might not agree with what you have in your cashbook. This is usually because you might not know of some of the charges your bank might have deducted from your account and you have not written them in your cashbook, or because your bank has not recorded some of your transactions at the time of issuing the bank statement.

To be sure everything is alright; you have to do something known as bank reconciliation at the end of every week/month/year. To do this, simply match all the transactions on your cashbook with what you have on your bank statement.

Use a pen to tick all the transactions that appear in your cashbook and in your bank statement. If a transaction is not in either of the books, you can investigate to see why. If it is not charging by the bank or interests, you should ask the bank for an explanation as to why the transaction is yet to reflect in your account so that they can correct it.

Chapter 5:

How to set up a Double-Entry Bookkeeping System for Your Business

Double-entry bookkeeping system, although more complicated to set up, shows a much more detailed account of the financial position and performance of your business.

To understand the double-entry system of bookkeeping, you need to understand something called the accounting equation.

The accounting equation is this:

Assets = Liabilities + Equity

Assets

Here, assets refer to anything that has a monetary value that the business owns. There are 5 different types of assets:

Current Assets: These include things owned by the bank for a short period such as cash, bank balances, money owed to the business, and short-term investments expected to mature within one year.

Fixed Assets: Fixed assets are physical/tangible properties owned by the business and usable for several years such as buildings, land, equipment, vehicles, furniture, fittings, and so on.

Inventory: Inventory is goods/products the business sells.

Long term Investments: Investments owned by the business such as bonds and stocks, but cannot yield or be converted into cash within a year.

Intangible Assets: Intangible assets are assets that are valuable to the business but cannot be seen or touched such as goodwill, trademarks, patents, and copyrights.

Liabilities

Liability refers to what the business owes. It is any financial obligation that the business is legally bound to fulfill such as cash owed to vendors or suppliers or loans owed by the business.

Liabilities can also further divide into current liabilities expected to be paid within a year, and long-term liabilities that may extend for more than one year.

Equity

Equity refers to the value of cash or assets the business owner introduces to the business. For instance, if you started your business with $5,000, that amount is the equity.

What the accounting equation displays is the fact that whatever assets your business currently owns is either financed by the capital you introduced for running the business, or by debts you incur for the sake of running the business.

The double-entry system of bookkeeping builds upon this foundation because every single transaction you undertake, whether it's a sales or purchase transaction, would affect both sides of the equation, which is where the term 'double entry' comes from.

There are six major steps involved in setting up a double-entry bookkeeping system for your business as seen below:

Create Chart of Accounts

Your chart of accounts is like a table of contents for your different ledgers: It's simply a list of all the names of accounts you use in your bookkeeping system. It is from this list that you would pick which journals to credit and which ones to debit when a transaction occurs.

Here is a sample chart of accounts you can use for your business.

Assets Account	Liability Accounts	Owner's Equity Account	Operating Revenue Accounts	Operating Expense Accounts	Non-operating Revenue and Expenses, Gains, and Losses
Cash	Mortgage Loan Payable	Capital Account	Revenues	Wages/Salaries	Interests
Accounts Receivable	Notes Payable	Owner's Drawings		Utilities	Profit/loss on sales of assets
Inventory	Unearned Revenues			Rent	
Supplies	Accounts Payable			Advertising	
Prepaid Insurance	Wages Payable			Telephone	
Land	Interest Payable			Transportation	
Buildings				Internet	
Accumulated Depreciation on Assets				Depreciation	

This is just an example. You have to create your own accounts based on your business transactions.

Start with the Source Documents

The source documents are the original records of your financial transactions. For example, if you obtain an invoice from a supplier for a transaction, this is the original record of the transaction, what we call the source document. Other examples of source documents include credit notes, debit notes, receipts and cash memos, pay in slips, vouchers, and so on.

You need to create a filing system for these source documents because you shall use them to post transactions in the next step.

Post Transactions in Your Journals

You shall have to post information from your source documents in what we call a journal. The journals help you record and classify all your financial transactions. Think of them as little diaries for summarizing your business'' daily activities.

Every transaction in your source documents would be taken and recorded in your journals. This recording process is called 'posting' in bookkeeping. Each record you make in your journals would have to be recorded twice in two separate ledgers. One journal would be credited and the other journal would be debited. The values posted in each of the accounts must be the same and there must not be even a cent difference.

Each journal usually comes with two sides, a debit and a credit side.

Cash Account [Asset Account]

	Debit	Credit
Accounts Payable	$1,000	

At this point, you have completed the double entry process for that transaction.

Let us look at a few more examples so we can be sure you now know how to post in your ledgers because once you get a hang of that, you are already bookkeeping pro.

Let's say your business decides to issue a check of $700 to pay out of your $1,000 debt, what happens? Your bank balance [Assets Account] would reduce and your liabilities would also reduce; how do you post?

You go back to your asset account and post the $700 on the credit side to reflect the decrease. However, this time, the transaction was not through cash but through the bank so the asset account affected would be the bank account, not the cash account and so you would have to post this in the bank ledger.

So, assuming you had a balance of $2,500 in your bank account before you issued the check, your bank account would look like this:

Bank Account [Asset Account]

	Debit	Credit
Balance brought forward	$2,500	
Accounts payable		$700

Then you go to your liabilities account to make sure is also reflects the fact that you have paid out of your debts and your liabilities have reduced.

Accounts Payable Journal [Liability Account]

	Debit	Credit
Cash Borrowed		$1,000

However, you have only completed one-half of the posting. You still have to show that you now have extra cash for your business.

Cash is an asset and from the table above, debit entries would show an increase in assets while credit entries would show a reduction. The extra $1,000 is an increase; where do you post this transaction? Well, you post on the debit side to show that there has been an increase in your assets!

Stationery Account [Expenses Account]

	Debit	Credit
Bank account	$200	

You would have to post every transaction in your source documents to their relevant journals using the double-entry system and you continue posting from your source documents to each journal until the end of the period when you need to balance out your accounts and generate your weekly/monthly/daily report.

Accounts Payable [Liability Account]

	Debit	Credit
Cash Borrowed		$1,000
Bank Account	$700	

Here is a summary of the steps involved in posting in your journals:

- **Step 1**: Which two accounts are affected by this transaction?
- **Step 2**: Was there an increase or decrease in the value of the accounts?
- **Step 3**: Check table for posting guideline
- **Step 4**: Post transaction appropriately.

Now, let's say you have decided to purchase stationery worth $200 using your bank account.

Step 1: The two accounts affected are the bank account [Asset account] and the stationery account [Expenses account].

Step 2: There was a decrease in the value of the bank account [because you spent $200 out of it to purchase stationery] and there was an increase in the value of your stationery account [because you just bought some more stationery]

Step 3: Decrease in assets go on the credit side and increase in expenses go on the debit side.

Step 4: Posting done as seen below

Sales Journal

	Debit	Credit

Debits are recorded on the left side of the journal, while credits are recorded on the right side of the journal. Whenever a transaction that would increase the value of an account occurs, it is recorded on the debit side while a transaction that would reduce the value of an account is recorded on the credit side.

How do you know which accounts to debit and which ones to credit?

The table below shows you how each account is affected by debit and credit entries.

	Debit	**Credit**
Assets	Increase	Decrease
Expenses	Increase	Decrease
Liabilities	Decrease	Increase
Owner's equity	Decrease	Increase
Revenues	Decrease	Increase

From the table above, you can see that posting transactions to the credit side of your asset account would reduce the value of the account while posting transactions to the debit side of your expenses account would increase the value of the account.

Very straightforward, right?

Let us take some examples:

Assuming your business borrows $1,000 cash on 30 November 2017, which two accounts would this transaction affect?

Cash account [Assets] and Accounts Payable [Liability account] because you have extra $1,000 on your hands but your liability has also increased.

So how do you post this?

You want to record that there has been an increase in your liabilities so you look at the table above. It says debit entries decrease the value of liabilities and credit entries increase it.

Since your liabilities have increased, where do you post your entry? You do it one the credit side to show that there has been an increase in liabilities of course!

Bank Account [Asset Account]

	Debit	Credit
Balance brought forward	$2,500	
Accounts payable		$700
Stationery		$200

Transfer Your Journal Entries to Your General ledger

When done with your journal entries, the next thing to do is to post the journal entries into your ledger account. In bookkeeping, we refer to the journal as the "book of original entry," while we refer to the general ledger as "book of final entry."

As you must have seen from the journals, we just record the transactions and there is no way to know what the balance in each account is at the end of each period. The ledger provides such information because unlike the journal, it has a balancing column.

Here is a sample of what your ledger would look like:

Date	Details	Reference Number	Debit $	Credit $	Balance $

To post from your journal to your general ledger, here are the steps to take:

- Step 1: Post each transaction from your journal to the ledger.

- Step 2: Find the balance on each account:
- For expense and asset category accounts, calculate the balance in each account by subtracting the amount in the credit side from the amounts in the debit side.
- For liability and equity accounts, calculate the balance in each account by subtracting the amounts in the debit side from the amounts in the credit side.

Examples are below:

Bank Account [Asset Account]

Date	Details	Reference Number	Debit $	Credit $	Balance $
1st Nov. 2015	Deposit		$5,000		
5th Nov. 2015	Rent			$200	
13th Nov. 2015	Deposit		$1,500		
21st Nov. 2015	Inventory			$2,500	
22nd Nov. 2015	Deposit		$500		
30th	Balance				$4,300

| Nov. 2015 | carried forward | | | | |

At the end of every period, your ledger would carry a balance amount for all the transactions in each account.

Create Your Trial Balance

After posting your ledgers, the next account to handle is your trial balance. The trial balance is simply a list of all balances extracted from your ledgers.

Its main use is to confirm the accuracy of all your accounts at the end of the year or period. If the total on either side of the account is not the same figure, it simply means there is a discrepancy somewhere in the account.

There are four major steps involved in creating a trial balance for your business:

- **Step 1:** Create three columns as seen below:

Account	Debit $	Credit $

- **Step 2:** Now, begin writing all the names of the accounts in your ledger. All balances in assets accounts should be posted under the debit column, all balances in liabilities accounts should be posted under the credit column, all balances in revenue account should be posted under the credit column, balances in expenses accounts should be under the debit column and equity balances should be posted under the credit column.

Example of the trial balance:

Account	Debit $	Credit $
Cash	$700	
Accounts Receivable	$300	
Office equipment and Supplies	$800	
Bank Loan		$500
Accounts Payable		$100
Rent Expense	$60	
Stocks		$1,000
Salaries	$250	
Supplies	$120	

Consulting Income		$700
Utilities	$70	
Total	**$2,300**	**$2,300**

- Step 3: **Add the balances on each side of the account.**
- Step 4: **The debits should equal the credits as seen above.**

Create Your Profit and Loss Accounts/Income Statement

At the end of each period, you want to know the financial performance of your business. This could be at the end of the month or at the end of the year, or any other period you choose.

The profit and loss statement tells you whether your business made profits or sustained losses at the end of each period. The profit and loss statement has two parts: The income part and the expenditure part.

The income part shows all the income your business generated including gross profit brought forward, revenue from sales, rent received, commissions received, and any other indirect income. The expenditure portion shows all the expenses that the business incurs as well as gross loss brought forward.

Step 1: Subtract all direct costs related to your income such as costs of transporting the goods to the buyer and costs of purchasing inventory from the sales amount. This gives you your gross profit amount.

Step 2: Subtract all operating expenses from your gross profit amount such as your costs of advertisement, wages, and salaries for your employees, rent, insurance, and every other expenses related to the operations of your business. This gives you your operating income.

Step 3: Subtract all other non-operating income, expenses and losses incurred by the business from your operating income. Losses from lawsuits or sales of assets or incomes from sales of investments are examples of items to go under this category. This gives a figure for your net income or net loss as the case may be.

Below is a format you can use to prepare your income statement:

Sample Income Statement for the Year Ended 31st December, 2016

	$	$
Sales		10,000
Less: Cost of Goods Sold		7,500

Gross Profit		2,500
Operating Expenses		
Office Equipment and Supplies Expenses	$600	
Advertising Expenses	$200	
Commissions Expenses	$500	
Less: Total Operating Expenses		$1,300
Operating Income		$1,200
Non-Operating or other interest revenues		
Interest revenues		$500
Gains on investment sales		$300
Interest expenses		[$50]
Non-operating losses		[$150]
Add: Total Non-Operating income		$600
Net Income		$1,800

Prepare Your Balance Sheet

The last account you have to prepare is your balance sheet. The balance sheet helps show the value of your assets, liabilities, and equity at the end of the period.

It helps you see what your business owes and owns at a glance. Below is the format for creating your balance sheet:

All the assets your business owns would go on the left side of the balance sheet, while all the liabilities and equity would go on the right side. Just like the trial balance, add each side of the balance sheet together and the figures on either side should be the same.

After preparing your balance sheet, you have successfully completed the bookkeeping process for the period. You can now present your financial reports to your management, or use it to prepare your tax filing documents as the case may be.

Chapter 6:

The Balance Sheet

A balance sheet is going to show the assets of the company, the liabilities of the company, and the net worth, or the owner's equity. The balance sheet will work along with the other financial documents that we have talked about in order to show a complete picture of the financial state of that company. If you hold onto stocks of that company, it is a good idea to understand more about the balance sheet, such as how it is structured, the best ways to look over and understand the sheet, and even tips for reading through the balance sheet.

How Can I Use this Financial Document?

The balance sheet is going to be split up into two parts. These two parts are going to be based on an equation, and they must either end up equaling each other or coming out so that they are balanced, or something is wrong with your numbers. The formula that is needed to work with the balance sheet will include:

Assets = Liabilities + Shareholder's Equity

What all this means is that all the assets, or the money used to operate the company, need to be balanced out by the financial obligations of the company, along with any of the equity investment that comes back to that company, and then they will be known as that company's retained earnings.

The assets are important because they are what the company will use in order to operate the business. The equity and the liabilities are going to be what will support those assets. The owner's equity, which can be known as the shareholder's equity, if the company is publicly traded, will include any of the money that the shareholders invested in that company. It can also include any retained earnings as well. This is important because it is going to represent the funding sources for that particular business.

One way that the balance sheet is different than the income statement we talked about before is that the balance sheet we talked about earlier is more of a snapshot that showcases the financial position of that company right then and there. If the accountant does this financial document on May 21, 2018, then the balance sheet will show where the company is on that date. It won't cover February 21 to May 21. It just shows May 21.

The Balance Sheet for the Securities and Exchange Commission

Just like the bank wants you to put together a balance sheet to take a look at whether they think you can do well with any credit they offer, the government is going to require that any company that is traded publicly will put together a balance sheet, usually each quarter, to show to their shareholders.

This balance sheet can be important because it will allow all potential and current investors to see a good snapshot of the finances of that company. In addition to some other things, the balance sheet is going to show you all the value of the stuff that the company owns, right down to the office supplies that the employees use, the amount of debt that the company is taking care of right now, and how much inventory is in the warehouse. It can even tell the investors about how much money the business will have available to work with through the short-term.

This balance statement is going to be one of the first financial statements that you should analyze when you want to see the value of the company. Before you can learn how to analyze this balance sheet, it is important to know how it is structured.

Before we get into this too much though, you need to understand that the limited partnership, limited liability Company, and the corporation balance sheets are going to be a lot different from the regular household balance sheet. This is mainly because these companies have a lot of complex items in their accounting records to keep the company going. This is why many of these companies rely on an accountant to help them get it done.

Businesses are often faced with many difficult questions that others may not know the answers to, such as how to depreciate out the costs for some of their business expenses, how to record the lease obligations, how to account for the expenses of construction at the power plan, and so much more.

No matter how overwhelming it can seem in the beginning to figure out all the different parts of the balance sheet, it is actually pretty simple once you have looked at a few. The best way to get through the balance sheet is to remember that the purpose of this financial statement is to answer three basic questions for anyone who is looking at that sheet. These three main questions that the balance sheet should answer include:

What does the company have? These will be the assets of the company.

What does the company owe on? These will be the liabilities of the company.

What is left over for the owners of that business if they were to pay off all their debts? This one is going to be the shareholder equity or the book value.

These are pretty advanced terms and fancy words, but they are there to help give the investor a good idea of where the business is at that time. If you can remember the objective of the balance sheet, all those fancy words and accounting complexities won't seem as overwhelming when you take a look over it later.

One thing to remember is that unlike some of the other financial statements, the balance sheet is not going to cover a range of dates. The information that is present in the balance sheet is going to be good as of the date that is on the balance sheet, but it won't be able to tell you any date ranges in the process. If you are looking to deal with this issue when calculating many of the accounting ratios, then the best way to do this is to work with the averagely weighted figures of the balance sheet.

An example of this is if you would like to figure out what the average value of inventory was for that year for the company. You would be able to do this by taking the value of the inventory at the previous yearend, add it to the inventory's value at the end of this year, and then divide them by two.

This is a quick trick that will help you to avoid any distortions by ending period figures that may or may not be able to accurately reflect what occurred throughout that year. For example, if the manufacturing business was able to pay off all the debt it had in the year and this showed that there was $0 in liabilities on this balance sheet, but then there was a line there to show the interest expense on your income statement, this could be confusing.

By taking the time to weigh the average debt outstanding from the balance sheet over that same period, you may be able to get a better idea of what the business has going on here and why they listed some interest costs on the income statement but not on the balance sheet.

What Are the Different Types of Assets?

Next, we need to take a look at some of the assets that the company needs to keep track of. Remember that these assets are going to help the company do its normal operations. There are two types of assets that each business will need to pay attention to including current assets and non-current assets.

Current Assets

Current assets are going to be any that the company owns that have a lifespan that is a year or less. This means that the asset has to be easily changed over to cash if the company needs to. Such assets will include inventory, accounts receivable, and cash or cash equivalents.

Cash, which is the most fundamental and most commonly thought about the current asset, can also include checks and bank accounts that are not restricted. Cash equivalents are going to be assets that are very safe, but which can also be turned into cash quickly if the company needs. The U.S. Treasury is a good example of this. And then there are the accounts receivables, which are going to show the reader any of the obligations that customers and others owe to the company over the short-term. These sometimes happen if a company allows the customer to use credit to purchase the product or service.

Inventory is an important current asset as well. Inventory can include things like the raw materials to make a product, the products that are still in the process of being created, and the finished goods. Each company is going to be different, and the exact way that the inventory account looks is going to be different. For a manufacturing firm, there may be a lot of raw materials, but a retained firm wouldn't have any raw materials.

Non-Current Assets

These non-current assets are going to be any that you are not able to turn into cash very easily, which the company doesn't plan to turn into cash soon. These also include items that will last more than a year. Tangible assets such as land and buildings are included in this. Sometimes, the intangible items will be added to this as well.

What Are the Different Liabilities?

Another part of the balance sheet is the liabilities. These are going to be any financial obligations that the company owes to an outside party. Similar to the assets above, these will fall under the idea of being either a current liability or one that will last long-term.

The long-term liabilities are going to be any of the debts that the company has that will be due in more than a year from that balance sheet date. The current liabilities though are going to be any liabilities that need to be paid off within a year. This could include some of the shorter-term borrowings or even the latest interest that you paid on a longer loan.

The company needs to properly list out all the liabilities that they have on this balance sheet. This helps the investor or the lender know how many debts and obligations that the company is dealing with, and then they can compare this to the profits of the company to see where the company stands financially. This information is much more important to making sound decisions for the investor or the lender compared to just looking at the profits.

For example, a company may have some great profits, but if they have such high debts that they can barely keep up with them, then those high profits don't mean anything. The investors and lenders want to make sure that the company is able to handle their debts and pay them off, while still making a profit and paying their investors before they put any money into it.

Shareholders' Equity

The shareholder's equity is going to be the beginning amount of money that the owners and others put into the business. If at the end of that year, the company wants to take their net earnings and reinvest it back into the company, then these earnings need to move over to your income statement and then placed into the equity account for the shareholder to make it work. This account is important because it will represent the net worth of the company.

The balance sheet is so important to a business. It gives a great snapshot of the finances of a business and can give analysts, investors, and lenders a good idea of where the business stands financially. Filling it out properly is going to make a big difference in how people view your company.

Chapter 7:

The Cash Flow Statement

The third document that needs to be found in the financial report of a business is the cash flow statement. This is going to be an important financial statement because it will showcase the amount of cash and cash equivalents that will enter or leave that company. This statement can also measure how well the company can manage its cash position. This means that it shows the capability of the company to earn money or cash and then put that money toward all the debts and other obligations that are needed to fund any expenses to keep the business going.

This statement will help finish out the financial statements of the company, along with the income statement and the balance sheet, and it is mandatory that all three of these documents are presented.

What ways can I use this statement?

There are a variety of reasons that this statement can help out a business. First, the cash flow statement is there to help any investor to understand how well the company is running its operations. It can also explain where the company is getting its money from and how they are spending that money. The cash flow statement is so important because it can be used to help investors determine how financially secure the company is at that time and whether it is a smart decision to invest with them.

Investors are not the only ones who can rely on the cash flow statement. Many creditors will use the cash flow statement to help determine how much cash is available. This is referred to as the liquidity of the company. This cash needs to be used to help the company fund any operating expenses that it has and pay off its debts.

The Structure of Your Cash Flow Statement

When an accountant designs a cash flow statement for any business, there are some components or categories that need to be present in this document for it to be complete. These four components include:

- Any cash the company gets from operating activities.

- Any cash that the company gets from its investing activities.

- Any cash that the company gets from financing activities.

- This category includes any activities that are non-cash. These are sometimes included, and it will depend on the rules found under GAAP, or the generally accepted accounting principles.

One thing to note here is that the cash flow statement is going to be different from the other financial documents that we talked about before. The main reason for this is because the cash flow statement is not going to have information about all cash that may happen in the future that is recorded as a credit. Because of this, cash is not going to be considered the same thing as net income.

Operating Activities

Now we need to break down the components of the cash flow statement so we know what needs to go into each part. The operating activities will be first. These operating activities found on the cash flow statement will be any sources as well as uses of cash from the business activities of that company. To make it easy, this is going to reflect how much cash that company is able to generate through doing business or offering their products and services to the customer.

Generally, any of the changes that the company makes in cash, depreciation, accounts payable, inventory, and accounts receivable can be reflected in cash from operations. Some examples of the operating activities of the company would include:

- Any payments for rent

- The payments you make for wages and salary to the employees.

- Payments that you make for suppliers for the services and goods that you use in production.

- Any tax payments you make on income.

- Any interest payments you make on loans or your mortgage.

- Receipts from any sales of the services or goods you sell.

When it comes to the trading portfolio, or if it is an investment company, it would have receipts about debt or equity instruments and receipts from the sale of a loan can be included. When you try to prepare this cash flow statement under the indirect method (we will talk about this method in a bit), things like deferred tax, any losses or gains that the company may get from assets that are noncurrent, amortization, depreciation, and dividends that come from the investment opportunities of the company and more can be included. However, with this indirect method, purchase or any sales of your long-term assets can't be counted under the operating activities.

How Can I Calculate My Cash Flow?

Now we need to learn how to calculate the cash flow of a company. The cash flow is going to be calculated simply by making certain adjustments to the net income for that company. You can do this by either subtracting or adding the differences in credit transactions, expenses, and revenue that come from any transaction that will occur between two accounting time periods. The numbers that you will use are found on several of the financial documents to help you get started.

These adjustments need to be made because there are some non-cash items that have been calculated into the net income (found on the income statement) as well as into the liabilities and the total assets (which is found on the balance sheet). So, since not all of your transactions are going to involve some actual cash items, then you need to re-evaluate some of the items to come up with an accurate number for cash flow from operations.

Because you have to go through and make some changes to get an accurate number, there are going to be two main methods that accountants can use to make sure that you are able to come up with the cash flow numbers. The two main methods are the direct and then the indirect method.

With the direct method, you are going to get all of your cash payments and receipts and add them up. This information can include cash that you paid to suppliers, cash that you paid to your employees for salaries and cash receipts from the customer. These figures are going to be calculated by using the end and the beginning balances from your different business accounts, and then you can check whether there is an increase or a decrease in the net amounts of these accounts.

You can also choose to work with the indirect method. In this method, the cash flow from all of your operating activities will be calculated. You will first take the net income off the income statement. Because this income statement for the company will be prepared on what is known as an accrual basis. When you use this method, the revenue for that company is only recognized at the time it is earned rather than at the time it is received.

Because of this information, the net income is not always the best representation of how the company's cash flow is doing. This is why you will need to go through and make some adjustments for any of the items that will affect your net income. Yes, the company is still waiting to receive cash for the product or service, but it still needs adjustment.

With the indirect method, you will also need to make adjustments to make sure that some of your non-operating activities are added back in. An example of doing this would be with depreciation. Since this depreciation of assets is not seen in most cases as a cash expense, it needs to be added back in with the total you receive on the net sales during that cash flow calculation. You only want to add this asset into your statement when it is time to sell it.

The amount that the account receivable decreases are then going to be added into the net sales is how many customers paid off their credit accounts that time period, and that number needs to be added to the net sales of the company.

But if there is an increase between one periods of accounting to another in the accounts receivable, then the amount needs to be deducted from your net sales. Even though the amounts are counted as revenue in the accounts receivable, they are not really cash, so it shouldn't show up on the cash flow statement.

The change in inventory is also another thing to go through and check on. When the company has an increase in the amount of inventory they have, it could signal that the company spent more of their money to purchase the raw materials that they need to make the products. If the inventory was paid off with cash, then the increase in this inventory needs to be taken from your net sales. A decrease in the amount of inventory that you have is added over to the net sales part of the statement. If you ended up purchasing some inventory and did so on credit, then you need to see an increase in the accounts payable section. Then you need to have the increased amount from the past year put in with the net sales.

This same process is going to work with other parts of your company as well. It could work for prepaid insurance, salaries payable, taxes payable, and more. If you pay something off, then you will subtract the difference in value that you owed from one year to the following one from the net income. But if you still have some that is owed on that item, then this difference needs to be added to the net earnings.

The Investing Activities and Your Cash Flow Statement

Some of the investing activities that the company partakes in can be used on the cash flow statement as well. Investing activities can be any source or any use of the cash from any investments the company participates in. These may include things like purchasing a new asset, loans that are made to a vendor, a loan that is received from customers, or any payments that the company receives because of an acquisition or a merger. In short, any changes that occur from investments, assets, or equipment will relate to the cash you have from investing.

In most cases, any changes in cash because of your investments are just going to end with cash out of the item, mostly because you took that cash and used it to purchase buildings, new equipment, or even some shorter-term assets, like a marketable security. However, if your company decides to divest an asset, then this transaction is going to be called cash in for helping you calculate your cash from investing.

Financing Activities and Your Cash Flow Statement

Cash that comes from the financing activities on your cash flow statement will include the sources of cash from investors or bank, and it can also include uses of cash that you paid out to the shareholders. Payments for repurchasing stocks, payment for dividends, and repayment of debts or loans can all be added to this category.

If you have some changes in cash from this financing, then you are cashing in whenever the capital rises, but then cashed out when the dividends are paid. So, if a company issues out a bond to the public, then the company will receive some cash for that financing. However, when they have to pay out some interest to the bondholders, the company will reduce the amount of cash that it has control over at that time.

Tying Together the Income Statement, the Balance Sheet, and the Cash Flow Statement

As we mentioned earlier in this chapter, the cash flow statement is going to rely on the balance sheet and the income statement to come up with the numbers that you will use in your calculations. You may need to make some changes to the numbers to get an accurate value, but if you filled out your balance sheet and your income statement properly, then you will have the information that you need to start on the cash flow statement.

Net earnings that are found in the income statement will be used as the figure for the cash flow statement. Without this information, or with the wrong information, then the information is going to show up wrong on the cash flow statement as well.

In regard to this balance sheet, your net cash flow is going be measurable as well. If the cash decreased or increased between your balance sheets, then the net cash flow needs to change the same amount, or something is wrong. So, if you are trying to come up with the cash flow for 2017, then you would use all the balance sheets from 2016 to 2017 to help you get the right information.

The cash flow statement is an important document, which is why it is included along with the other financial documents for a company. This statement is going to measure the strength, the profitability, and the outlook over the long-term for the company. The cash flow statement can help an investor, a manager, and others determine whether the company has enough cash and that the cash is liquid enough to pay off its expenses. A company can often rely on this cash flow statement to predict how their cash flow might be at a future time, which can be so important when they are working on things like budgeting for the future of that company.

For investors, the cash flow statement is a major tool that investors and managers like to work with. Since the cash flow statement is going to reflect the financial health of the company, since it is typical that when a company has more cash, then the better off they are doing. However, there are some times when this rule doesn't really work for the business. For example, there are times when a company will have a negative cash flow because of the growth strategy they chose. If the company expands its operations, it may eliminate some of its cash flow, but it will quickly gain those back and more once the operations are up and running.

When an investor takes the time to study the cash flow statement, the investor is going to get one of the best pictures of how much cash the company is able to generate. They get a good understanding of how financially secure the company is at that time. And it can help them to choose whether or not they want to invest in that company.

Chapter 8:

Tax Accounting

No matter what kind of business you run, there will come a time when you need to file your taxes. In your first year, you may not need to do this as you get things organized and up and running. But after that, or once you owe $1000 or more to the IRS if you are a sole proprietorship, then you will need to pay your taxes each quarter.

Having accurate records and filling out the income statement, the balance sheet, and the cash flow statement can make it easier to do your taxes. You can just insert the numbers into your tax forms, and you can use this information to help you get the deductions to save you even more.

With the help of your accountant, you will be able to take all of the documents that you have and get your tax documents all set up and ready. Let's take a look at tax accounting, how it works, and why it is so important to your business to get this done.

What Is Tax Accounting?

Tax accounting is a subset of accounting. It is going to focus on preparing and handling taxes rather than the public financial statements of the company. Tax accounting is going to be governed by the Internal Revenue Code, which will dictate the specific rules that all individuals and companies need to follow when they work on their tax returns.

Tax accounting is a basic means of accounting to help get taxes done. It can actually apply to everyone, including corporations, business, individuals, and other entities. Even those who have exemptions for paying taxes need to do some tax accounting. The purpose of this kind of accounting is to be able to track the funds of the company, including those that go out and those that come in, associated with entities and with individuals.

Having proof of all this information can be really helpful at tax time. Even if your income was small enough, or you had enough deductions or both to not pay taxes, it is going to be helpful to have a record of all the funds coming in and out of your business. You can keep track of how your business is doing and can prove your income if you are ever audited in the future.

The Tax Principles vs. GAAP

If you own a business or do accounting in the United States, you will notice that there are going to be two main sets of principles that can be used. These two rules are different, and you should not confuse them. The first is going to be principles that are used specifically in tax accounting, and the second ones will be for a financial account in general.

Under the rules of GAAP, all companies will need to follow a common set of procedures, standards, and principles in their accounting any time that they compile a financial statement and with all of their financial transactions. The GAAP rules will list out all the rules that you need to follow in order to write your balance sheets, income statement, and cash flow statement. There are various different rules that you will need to follow with GAAP, and it ensures that companies are going to record their financial information and that there is some unity between the financial statements.

While accounting is going to have a little bit to do with all of the financial transactions, tax accounting is going to focus all its energy on transactions that will affect the tax burden of a company, and how those items will relate to proper tax calculations and preparation with tax documents.

Tax accounting has some regulations placed on it and is regulated by the IRS to make sure that all of the tax laws are followed by individual taxpayers and tax accounting professionals. The IRS is also going to use specific documents and forms so that you can submit the tax information properly as the law requires from you.

Tax Accounting and How It Works for an Individual

Tax accounting can work for both individuals and for businesses. First, we are going to look at tax accounting and how it works for an individual. As an individual who pays taxes, tax accounting is going to focus mostly on items like the income of the individual, the deductions that they qualify for, any investments that they earned or lost on, and some other transactions that will affect how much you pay taxes.

This is a good thing because it is going to help limit the amount of information that individuals need to manage to finish their tax return. You don't have to go through and keep receipts of every transaction that you make for example. If you make a big purchase, you keep that receipt, but a grocery store trip isn't one that you need to keep track of at all. This makes it easier for most individuals to get their tax returns done without all the work.

With general accounting, the individual would have to go through a lot more work. General accounting would mean that you need to track all the funds that come in and then go out of the person's possession, no matter what the purpose. If you got some clothes, you would have to write that on the tax return. If you went out to eat, you would have to write that out as well. You would have to write out everything that is a personal expense even if those expenses had no tax implications.

With tax accounting, you only have to keep track of a few things for the year. You keep track of any income that you make either from investments, from a job or other sources. And then you keep track of the items that can be deducted from your taxes to reduce your tax burden. And then that is it.

Tax Accounting for a Business

Businesses are often going to benefit the most from tax accounting. Tax accounting is going to help a business to keep track of everything that it needs to use for tax purposes. It can also help them to get as many tax deductions as possible in order to save them money.

From the perspective of a business, more information needs to be analyzed to finish the process for tax accounting. While the company needs to track its incoming funds and earnings, similar to what the individual has to do, there is also another level of complexity that comes with business tax accounting. This comes with outgoing funds that are directed toward the obligations of the business.

There are a lot of different parts that the business needs to keep track of for tax accounting. This sometimes includes funds that are directed toward specific expenses of the business, or the funds that are directed out to the shareholders of the business.

While a business doesn't have to use a tax accountant to do these duties, many larger organizations will have one. Tax accounting is going to be pretty complex. The larger your business is the more complex the tax accounting process will be and having a tax accountant can help make this easier.

How Tax Accounting Works for Organizations Exempt from Taxes

There are some entities or businesses that are going to be exempt from taxes. Even in these instances, the business will need to perform tax accounting. This is mainly due to the fact that all businesses need to file an annual term. This is true no matter how much they owe in taxes and even if they are tax-exempt for the year.

These businesses will need to provide information that is in regard to their incoming funds, such as any donations or grants that the business gets. They will then need to explain how they will use these funds to help them operate during the year.

The point of doing this is to ensure that these businesses are following all the regulations and laws that govern the way that a tax-exempt business can run and operate. Even though these businesses will not end up having to pay any taxes, regardless of how much they make during the year, it is important to fill out the return and keep track of the information. This can show the IRS that you are using all your funds properly.

Tax accounting can be a difficult part to work on. There are a lot of rules and regulations that a business must adhere to and making sure that everything is filed right with the IRS is important. Hiring a tax accountant can make it easier to get this done without running into trouble at the end of the year.

Chapter 9:

The Cost Principle

The cost principle (or the cost constraint, to be more correct) is the last of the officially-recognized generally accepted accounting principles - but not in any way the least important one.

We have just briefly touched upon a concept similar to the cost principle in this book. Earlier, we said that when the costs of abiding by generally accepted accounting principles are too high, accountants have the possible option of omitting them.

The cost principle, also known as the cost/benefit principle or the cost/benefit constraint, states that the cost of providing information in your financial statements should be compared to the benefits of providing that information.

Now, this is a pretty tricky concept to grasp, precisely because it could lead to accountants and management to be tempted to omit certain negative information from their statements, stating that the information was too expensive to research and put together, as compared to the benefits of doing it.

It is, however, extremely important that you understand this constraint. Together with the materiality constraint, they lie at the very foundation of both generally accepted accounting principles and the constraints associated with them.

The cost benefit principle was not always followed. In the past, accountants informally tried to create some sort of balance between the cost of providing information and the practicality of doing it. However, today, a lot of businesses apply the cost benefit constraint - so they analyze the benefits of providing certain types of information in their financial statement and measure it against the cost of doing it.

The Issue with the Cost Principle

The cost/benefit principle is, like all generally accepted accounting principles, simple in theory. But it can get very complicated when you go in-depth and try to apply it to real life situations.

The cost part of the cost benefit principle is easy. You pretty much just have to analyze the costs of collecting, researching, putting together, processing, analyzing, storing, auditing, and sharing data.

When it comes to the benefit part of the same principle, however, things can get very tricky, because it is difficult to quantify it. For instance, if the information you want to provide an investor will offer them the chance for an accurate assessment of the company's financial situation, this is clearly a benefit and the information should be included. However, it is difficult to assign an actual value (numerical value, for that matter) to this benefit.

This entire issue makes the application of the cost/benefit principle a judgment call on the side of the accountants handling the situation. At all times, the concept of transparency should be applied, though - which means that you should not use the cost/benefit principle in an abusive way, to maneuver financial statements to the company's major advantage.

Is the Cost Principle Applied at All Times?

No, the cost benefit constraint is not to be applied on all types of financial reports. The ones the cost benefit principle applies to are very clearly stipulated in the accounting standards - and in all of the situations excluded from that list, all of the financial data should be reported regardless of what the costs associated with this might be.

In reality, very few types of information are actually expensive to acquire and this means that there is a very small number of situations when accountants are allowed to actually forego and avoid reporting a situation.

The cost benefit constraint is there to help bookkeepers and management keep everything transparent and efficient for the company. It is, however, one of the generally accepted accounting principles you are not very likely to use very often, precisely because it is very well-constrained itself as well. Use it cautiously and always check with the official accounting standards when in doubt!

Chapter 10:

Alternatives to GAAP and Everything They Imply

In the beginning of the book, we were discussing the fact that, although rule-based, generally accepted accounting principles method has their flaws and that they are not always useful for companies who want to provide the best and most reliable information to financial statement readers.

Within the body of generally accepted accounting principles, there is, however, a pretty fascinating world flourishing: the alternative GAAP. Or, in other words, rules and guidelines that has derived from the GAAP, extending their force beyond that, and based on real-life situations that have pushed accountants into going farther with their interpretation of a system that was, at least initially, conceived to be **uninterruptable.**

As a disclaimer, this chapter is going to be a long and winding one. We have thus far exposed the main generally accepted accounting principles and helped you understand what they really stand for.

From here on, we will dive deeper into the exceptions to those rules, how they happen, and what solutions there might be for them.

Keep in mind, though: the following subchapters of this **Accounting Principles** book do not serve as a day to day guide in accounting for companies who are large, public, or simply fit into the GAAP in terms of how they create their financial statements.

The following subchapters have two main purposes: to show that although rule-based, the GAAP allows for additional concepts to be added to the appendix body of generally accepted accounting principles AND to show you just how madly fascinating accounting can be when we go beyond entries, numbers, subtractions, and additions.

So, without further ado, let us proceed.

Are Alternative GAAP Methods Misleading?

This is, by far, one of the single most important questions when it comes to alternatives to generally accepted accounting principles. In the end, all of the accounting principles exist with the sole purpose of making financial reporting more transparent, especially for users of the financial reports.

Alternative GAAP methods might be, thus, considered to be misleading in some situations. However, further talk needs to be done on this topic, especially since alternative GAAP methods and adjacent GAAP rules might actually prove useful in a wide variety of contexts.

To understand how these GAAP alternatives might be misleading, we will first dive into some of the most commonly used methods:

1. Earnings before interest and taxes (also known as EBIT)

2. Earnings before interest, taxes, depreciation, and amortization (EBITDA)

3. Adjusted earnings

In general, all methods that are not comprised by the GAAP are considered to be alternative. These methods are used when generally accepted accounting principles cannot convey nuances that might help financial statement readers gain a deeper understanding of a company's financial status and where it goes.

When companies feel the need to supplement (and this is a keyword!) the GAAP financial reporting with alternative methods, they often use it outside of financial statements per se, to describe items that are non-recurrent, but might affect the way a potential investor and creditor sees the company.

Non-GAAP methods are not standardized, so it is of the utmost importance for companies to have a very well-established set of controls and procedures that will help them make sure these measures are properly and accurately disclosed. These controls and procedures also help companies comply with the rules and regulations enforced by the SEC.

To establish these controls and procedures, companies must turn their attention to the following areas:

1. Compliance. All non-GAAP methods have to comply with the rules, regulations, and guidance enforced by the SEC.

2. Consistency. All non-GAAP methods must be presented in a consistent way, each accounting period. All the adjustments that are non-GAAP should be evaluated and applied in an appropriate and consistent way.

3. Data reliability. All the data used for the non-GAAP measures must be reliable at all times.

4. Calculation accuracy. All non-GAAP measures have to be flawlessly calculated.

5. Transparency. When non-GAAP measures are being used, they have to be fully, clearly, and unambiguously disclosed.

6. Management review. If non-GAAP methods must be applied, they have to be reviewed and confirmed by the management of the company, to ensure that they are appropriate.

7. Audit and management monitoring. When non-GAAP measures are used, they are fully disclosed, and their disclosure is closely monitored by the senior management of the company, as well as by the auditing committee.

How to Disclose Non-GAAP Measures

When your company has to use non-standard accounting methods, they have to be fully and transparently disclosed in financial statement appendixes.

One of the most important parts of this process is about involving the management of the company in it. In some situations, this only needs to be done with a disclosure committee, in other situations, it has to be done with the audit committee and in other situations, and it has to be done with the involvement of both of these committees.

SEC regulations state that all companies should consider creating a written policy to describe the nature of the adjustments to GAAP that are allowed and the actual non-GAAP measures to be used. Furthermore, companies should also explain the changes they have made that will influence inputs, calculations, and adjustments.

A disclosure committee should assist the CEO, CFO, and the audit committee in creating and monitoring disclosures - including, but not limited to non-GAAP methods that might be used. In most cases, the disclosure committee is formed out of management - but in some cases, companies might allow the disclosure committee to function as a sub-branch of the board.

Such a policy might describe any or all of the following:

1. A qualitative description of the adjustments made that are non-recurring;

2. A quantitative description of the thresholds at which any kind of income or expenses have to be evaluated to determine if they should or shouldn't be included in the non-GAAP adjustments.

As you can see, even when non-GAAP methods are used, they have to be internally regulated and they also have to be fully disclosed to external readers of the financial statements.

Can the use of non-GAAP measures still be confusing and maybe even intentionally misleading in this case?

Well, yes. Given that the drafting and the disclosure of these methods happen internally, they could be used to put a company in a better light than it actually is. The SEC had been closely monitoring the use of non-GAAP methods since 2016, and an internal task force has been created with this purpose.

Whenever possible, try to avoid non-GAAP measures - they can be misleading indeed, and they can be very complicated to draft as a disclosure statement. They can, at times, prove useful as well - so, again, it is all a matter of judgment calls you have to make as an accountant.

Contemporary Debate against Non-GAAP

The Enron scandal happened more than 17 years ago but to date, it lingers as one of the most prominent and notable financial scandals of the United States of America. Back then, the SEC urged for the creation of rules for non-GAAP measures.

A little over two years ago, in 2016, the lack of regulation for non-GAAP methods was put under scrutiny once again - this time, in a Valeant Pharmaceuticals case that reminded the whole world of the Enron situation at the beginning of the 2000s. As with Enron, Valeant was not fully honest in their financial statements - and they are paying dearly for this.

On the surface, many things have changed since the Enron scandal that urged American authorities toward better regulations. However, the Valeant Pharmaceuticals case proves that there is still a lot of leeway and that companies still practice dubious financial statement methods, most of which are at least somewhat fueled by the non-GAAP methods.

You might be tempted to think that not a lot of companies do the same - but in reality, even companies that abide by the generally accepted accounting principles still find loopholes they can use to manipulate the numbers. Studies show that this happens a lot more frequently than we might believe.

In themselves, non-GAAP methods are not **inherently bad**. Their existence is allowed precisely because GAAP can be, at times, flawed. In the hands of irresponsible and dishonest companies and executives, however, these non-GAAP methods can turn into a real tool of manipulation and misinformation - and yes, this hurts investors **a lot**.

Take, for example, the issue of performance-based bonuses. They have been tax deductible for more than twenty years (nearly thirty) now - and companies frequently compensate executives this way. Most of the time, however, reporting these compensations are tightly knit to non-GAAP metrics that are created in a way that executives always reach their targets.

Consequently, executives are very tempted to maneuver non-GAAP methods in any way they can, so that they can reach their target. For instance, if a company reports restructuring as a non-recurring charge, this would be done through a non-GAAP method. However, regulation is unclear as to how many times this can be done - so if the company does it for two years in a row, there should be something suspicious there (because those charges can hardly be considered as "non-recurring", given that they have happened for so many years in a row).

Similar tactics are used all over the financial world. While we are not saying that these methods are inefficient, we are saying that they are very unethical and that, once the problem explodes, it can lead to severe legal issues for you as an individual helping with the manipulation and for your company as well.

How Common Accounting Concepts Connect to GAAP and Alternatives to GAAP

As established in the first chapters of this book, generally accepted accounting principles are rules that have to be followed by the accounting community (in this case, because these are the US GAAP, the rules have to be followed by accountants in the United States of America).

Up until now, we have gone through the most important rules of accounting - generally accepted accounting principles - and described their purpose and their use.

To help you gain an even better understanding of what these rules are all about, we will now put them through the lens of some of the most essential accounting terms:

Revenue Recognition

It is important to know when revenue should be recognized, because, according to the basics of different types of accounting, this happens at different times, influencing when it should be entered onto balance sheets.

Here are the instances when revenue recognition should occur:

1. When goods are sold or services are rendered (in accrual accounting);
2. When cash is collected - either through installments or through the cost-recovery-first method (in cash accounting);
3. When the production or construction of a product begins (in the percentage-of-completion method of accounting, usually applied in the case of long-term contracts);
4. When a customer's return time expires (if your business allows customers to return products in a given amount of time after purchase).

In general, recognizing revenue at the time of production will lead to reports with a large cumulative income and assets - and this is closely followed by the recognition of revenue when a sale happens.

It is worth mentioning, however, that the revenue recognition model that produces the largest earnings will vary a lot, depending on the accounting period, and the specificities of a business in general.

Generally speaking, companies that are on a growing path will report the largest earnings when they record their revenues when production or construction happens. Companies that are on a decline, however, will report the largest earnings when they make their recognition at the time of cash collection. Steady firms (that don't grow or decline) will usually report more or less the same earnings, accounting period after accounting period.

Please note that regardless of the revenue recognition method and accounting method you have chosen, this will only affect the timing and not the amount of revenue itself. Does this have an impact on financial statements? Yes, somewhat - in the sense that if your statements are released right after a surge in sales, they might not be 100% accurate. Accounting standards do seem to allow this, however - and accountants have quite a lot of freedom when it comes to choosing their accounting method.

In some cases, recognizing the revenue when it happens (e.g. when goods or services are sold, such as in accrual accounting) is the better option. However, if you run a company that will conduct operations over the course of multiple years to deliver one project (e.g. a construction company), you will find that the percentage-of-completion method suits them better.

Uncollectible Accounts

This concept has been touched upon in our previous chapters - but we want to dive a little deeper into it because it can be very complex. Of course, this is the kind of concept that would take an entire separate book (to say the least) to explain - but we will try to provide you with a little more information here, for the purpose of a better understanding of accounting principles in general.

A firm can recognize an expense as uncollectible in two moments: the accounting period when it recognizes the revenue (such as in the allowance method) or in the accounting period when the discovery that the collection of specific accounts cannot happen is made (such as in the direct write-off method).

The first method will usually result in the smallest earnings and assets on the balance sheet. The reason this happens is because it recognizes the bad debt earlier than the other method mentioned above.

The method showing the largest cumulative assets and earnings depends on each business and the specificities of their operations. However, it is very important to note that GAAP requires accountants to use the allowance method if the uncollectible amounts are predictable. At the same time, however, the income tax legislation in the United States requires firms to use the direct write-off method when it comes to tax reporting.

Inventories

In general, companies report their inventories using the lower side of the acquisition cost or market value. However, there are instances when a company cannot or simply doesn't want to specifically identify which of the goods in its inventory it has sold - and in such situations, a cost flow assumption is made.

There are multiple types of cost flow assumption models - such as FIFO, LIFO, or weighted average. IASB will generally prefer the FIFO or weighted average method because they tend to be more accurate. For instance, in the case of FIFO, the largest earnings and assets of a company's valuations will be recorded when the acquisition costs increase - and the lowest earnings and assets will be reported when the acquisition costs decrease.

LIFO, on the other hand, works the exact opposite way, showing the smallest earnings and assets when the acquisition cost is boosted and the highest earnings when they decline. This makes LIFO the least conservative method of doing inventory, and thus it makes it less GAAP-compliant as well.

Generally speaking, if only very small changes in acquisition costs occur, the earnings and assets valuations will not be reported much differently. However, the more rapid the rate of inventory turnover is, the more you will reduce the difference between the three methods of cost flow assumptions.

Last, but not least, it is important to note that in most cases, accountants have quite a lot of freedom in selecting the types of cost flow assumption methods they want to use. It is also worth mentioning that in the United States, firms are obliged to use LIFO in financial reporting if they are using it for tax reporting as well.

Depreciable Assets

Machinery, equipment, as well as other depreciable assets has a special way of being treated from an accounting point of view.

Companies are allowed to depreciate fixed assets using different methods: the straight line, the declining balance, the sum of the year's digits method, or the units of production method.

In some parts of the world, tax reporting has been playing a very important role in setting the acceptable accounting standards (such as Germany or France, for example). In those countries, firms are more inclined to use accelerated depreciation methods for the purpose of financial reporting.

In other countries, however, where different accounting methods are used for tax reporting (such as the UK and the USA, for instance), accountants are more inclined to use the straight-line method. This method will normally provide the largest earnings and asset valuations, while the sum of the years' digits is next in line from this point of view.

When the acquisition costs of any of the depreciable assets are at least somewhat stable and when the companies maintain their investment levels in these products or services, the depreciation methods mentioned before will produce similar balance sheets.

Accountants are allowed to use different estimates when it comes to the life expectancy of depreciable assets - mostly because the intensity of the use and the maintenance/repair policies could affect the age at which these assets are considered depreciated.

In most parts of the world, income tax laws do not require conformity between the different taxes methods used to report depreciable assets. There are, however, some exceptions to the norm.

Asset impairment is a concept adjacent to asset depreciation. All firms have the obligation to test their depreciable assets when an event suggests that their estimation of the fair value of the asset has declined. For instance, if your company has 50 laptops it has depreciated over the next 5 years, but two of them break unexpectedly, you should consider an asset impairment evaluation.

In the US, this compares the undiscounted cash flow that was initially estimated from the asset and their book value. If the latter exceeds the first, the asset impairment is official. The firm is then supposed to measure the impairment loss by comparing the fair value (market value or the present value of the expected cash flow associated with that asset) and the book value. The excess amount resulting from this calculation is considered to be the amount of the impairment loss.

Leases

If you run a company that uses property rights acquired on lease, you can record this in multiple ways. You can record the lease as an asset (and thus, be able to amortize it through the capital lease method) or you can recognize the lease transaction only when the company uses the asset, making payments each accounting period (and this is called the "operating lease method").

If you are the lessor in this situation, you can use the same methods. You can use the capital lease method (in which you set up the rights to receive the lease payments at the beginning of the lease) or you can use the operating lease method (in which you recognize the lease when you have already become entitled to receive the lease payments each accounting period).

Each lease situation is different and the two methods described above provide advantages and disadvantages, depending on the particular situation. In general, both the lessor and the lessee will use the same method for their lease contract, so that they can apply the same criteria from a capital vs. operating point of view. At the same time, however, the lessor and the lessee don't have to coordinate their accounting methods as well.

As you can see, all the aforementioned situations described in this subchapter are based on basic generally accepted accounting principles - but the situations and the complexity of the concepts has determined that new, adjacent rules should be applied.

These are just some examples - in reality, the alternatives to GAAP can get even harsher and they can produce even more intricate situations. In the end, however, this is part of the beauty of accounting: it may be a discipline dealing in numbers, but it can be very complex and very much based on analysis and judgment calls as well!

Understanding How the Standards Are Set

In every country, there is a body of accounting professionals that have the authority to select, draw, and establish the main accounting principles bookkeepers of all kinds must follow when preparing the financial statements within that given country.

Normally, you'd say yes, this is the right way to do it. There must be a standardization committee in charge of establishing what must or mustn't be done.

And you'd be right.

But going deeper than that will reveal a pretty big issue: how is that board of specialists itself being set and how does it operate?

Should the government be in charge of it, or should a body of private-sector professionals be dealing with this?

Should there be any degree of flexibility in the way they establish the rules and in the way they are applied, or should this be uniform at all times? What is the most efficient way to measure the economic results of a company's activities?

Should it all be rule-based or principle-based?

These are all important questions - questions that are still very much debated (as I have shown in the beginning of this book, for example, when I briefly touched upon the advantages and disadvantages of both the rule-based and the principle-based systems).

In the United States, the US Congress is the absolute, ultimate authority when it comes to establishing the acceptable accounting principles in America. This task is normally delegated to the SEC (Securities and Exchange Commission), which is a federal government agency. In their own turn, the SEC generally accepts everything the FASB (the Financial Accounting Standards Board) deems as acceptable accounting principles.

On the surface, the standard setting process in the US resides in the private sector. In reality, however, both the SEC and FASB communicate on every issue that might arise. The very proof of this is that FASB founded the EITF (Emerging Issues Task Force) when it was asked by the SEC to do so. This task force's purpose is to deal with any kind of reporting issues in cases where FASB has not issued any kind of statement just yet.

For a bit more background, we will reinstate the fact that most accounting firms in the US have some sort of flexibility in choosing their accounting principles - to some extent, of course. While in some instances the specific situation associated with a transaction a company has to record dictates the accounting method that is to be used, there are also cases when a wide degree of flexibility is applied, allowing companies to choose alternative methods.

"Constrained flexibility" is frequently used to describe accounting principles in the US On the one hand, the government recognizes that their goal (raising tax revenues) is different from the goal of their users who read financial reports (understanding them at their true value and being able to compare and contrast them). This is why the SEC and FASB have been assigned with the task of setting the standards.

When they select accounting principles, FASB takes two main elements into consideration: making deductions from all general principles **and** detailing the rules when this is needed.

It is important to note that their main methodology does not always give FASB the best and clearest guidance when it comes to the alternative methods the accountants might have to use when recording a transaction or event.

On top of this, lobbying companies might also incline FASB towards one side or another, arguing that they cannot apply certain methods in a cost-efficient way (which comes in contradiction to the cost benefit principle of GAAP itself). Furthermore, they sometimes claim that using generally accepted accounting principles will eventually disrupt decisions taken within their company and their capital markets as well.

There were instances when, under the pressure of lobbyists, FASB decided on specific standards, only to come back to them when regulators and academics flagged the standards as unethical or unprofessional for accountants.

This proves that the entire standard setting process in the United States (in accounting, and, most likely, in many other areas) is heavily influenced by politics and in itself, holds a political nature as well.

Governmental agencies in other countries to have a very powerful role in establishing the accounting standards to be used in those countries (such as Germany, Japan, or France, for example). However, the different ways in which these different standards have been set, changed, and influenced has led to accounting standards that are quite different from the United States.

As shown here, the accounting standard setting process is far from perfect. It has its flaws, and it has mishaps as well. However, because multiple institutions and professionals are watching over the entire standard setting process, it is far more unlikely that anything will slip through, allowing companies to make a grave error (intentional or not).

On the one hand, there is the governmental agency guarding over everything the private body does. On the other hand, there are the external professionals who might trigger a red flag when lobbyists push towards standards that would only benefit specific businesses, and not the entirety of the business community or the government in any way (e.g. standards that would allow for too much leeway in tax deductions would not have a long life).

The process of setting accounting standards is long and winding - and this is a perfect explanation of **why** it takes so long to come up with a body of accounting standards that is at least somewhat universally accepted.

Communication, in this sense, is being made - and with so many businesses expanding across the borders of the countries they were initially founded in, it makes perfect sense that an agreement will be reached - if not soon, then **at some point** in the future.

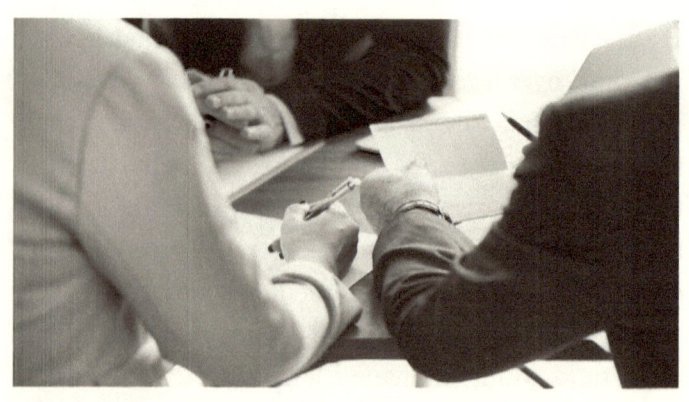

How Are the Alternatives to GAAP Used?

As mentioned before, most of the time, GAAP and IFRS standards are the best ways for businesses to do their bookkeeping and financial reporting. These standards are all there for a purpose: to help businesses make sure that they all play by the same rules and create the kind of financial statements that can be easily followed, compared, and analyzed.

As also shown before, these accounting standards can pose issues sometimes - and most often, this happens with small and medium-sized businesses (SMBs). The debates on alternative accounting standards and the results these debates have led to have, however, helped SMBs a lot in this respect.

In fact, institutions have gone so far as to develop a set of alternative standards called Other Comprehensive Basis of Accounting (created by the

American Institute of Certified Public Accountants and the International Accounting Standards Board). This newer set of guidelines and rules offers small and medium-sized businesses standards that are easier to adopt on their end. On the investors' and lenders' end, more and more of them become accustomed to and accept these new standards.

To put into perspective, the IFRS for SMBs is more simplified than the US GAAP. By comparison, the first has 230 pages, while the latter has no less than 20,000 pages of information.

The main challenge of these new (or alternative) standards is for both accountants and the finance community to learn how to adapt the methods that are currently used to these new standards. While in many countries, these standards are already deemed legitimate and acceptable, there is still much debate over whether or not everyone should move to the simpler, more concise standards.

It makes sense why so many have doubts. Until now, with some exceptions (some of which have grown into fully-fledged financial scandals), GAAP and extensive sets of standards have proved useful. So it is perfectly natural for all the players on the other side of the fence (bankers, investors, credit-rating agencies, and so on) would be wary in the case of a an oversimplification of the standards already set in place - mostly because it could lead to severe gaps and misinterpretations in the companies' financial statements.

On the other hand, a separate set of standards for small and medium businesses means that the accounting for their goodwill, investments, business combinations and other similar issues would be more simplified.

Given the explanation we have given in the previous subchapter on the intricacies of the standard-setting process, it is likely that quite a lot of time will pass before special standards for SMBs will be actually accepted at a unanimous level. It would, however, help these small and medium-sized businesses grow at a better, healthier pace, focusing on actual growth, rather than reporting standards, while still being able to access the help provided by investors and creditors.

Other Comprehensive Basis of Accounting

As mentioned before, the American Institute for Certified Public Accountants has developed a set of accounting standards meant for businesses who cannot (for one reason or another) comply with generally accepted accounting principles. This set of standards comes under the name of "other comprehensive basis of accounting" (or OCBOA).

The other comprehensive basis of accounting standards includes rules on how financial statements should be prepared in the absence of GAAP (but based on arguments that are supported in popular specialty literature). Furthermore, these rules also include a different basis of accounting (statutory) - one that is frequently used by insurance companies to comply with the commissions of state insurance.

Preparing your financial statements under OCBOA has two main advantages:

- The result will be generally easier to understand than statements created following GAAP (which, quite frankly, can be very intricate);

- The costs associated with preparing a financial statement under OCBOA is usually significantly smaller than that of preparing a financial statement under GAAP.

OCBOA and GAAP have the same purpose: that of helping accountants produce financial statements that are transparent and clear for their users. One of the main differences between the systems is that according to the other comprehensive basis of accounting rules, cash flow statements are not required.

There is, as you would expect, quite a lot of criticism surrounding OCBOA - and one of the main points critics bring up is connected to the fact that disclosures are not properly made. Thus, specialists recommend that a very comprehensive disclosure should be made by any business that is using the other comprehensive basis of accounting rules, so that financial statement readers get a full, clean, and understandable picture of that company's financial records. Comprehensive disclosures should include all the details needed for the understanding of financial statements - including, but not limited to, the basis of accounting used, any kind of risks, uncertainties, and contingent liabilities as well.

What Is Considered OCBOA?

According to the US Statement on Auditing Standards, it can be considered as "other comprehensive basis of accounting" in any of the following situations:

- Using a statutory basis of accounting (such as in the example given above, with the basis of accounting used by insurance companies);

- Cash-basis financial statements, as well as modified-cash-basis statements too;

- Financial statements on an income tax basis;

- Any financial statements that have been produced using support from specialty literature, which is then applied throughout the entirety of the financial statement and the material items appearing in it.

There are a number of situations when OCBOA statements are preferred, for a variety of reasons. These situations include:

- Cases when a GAAP statement is not necessary because of the loan covenants;

- Cases when a GAAP statement is not needed because of regulatory circumstances;

- Cases when businesses focus on who the users of financial statements are and what they want to see from the financial statements (e.g. cases when the financial statement is required by regulatory agencies);

- Cases when the company needs to reduce the cost of financial statements and audits (as OCBOA-based statements are, as mentioned before, simpler and less expensive to produce).

It is extremely important to note the fact that, indeed, the other comprehensive basis of accounting rules are quite different from generally accepted accounting principles. They are, however, guided by a code as well. This code includes rules such as:

- All professional accounting standards are still applicable to OCBOA-based financial statements;

- There must be a disclosure of the basis of accounting needed;

- The statements must be titled in a way that draws a clear distinguishable line between them and the titles of statements created based on GAAP;

- OCBOA statements can still be audited. Furthermore, they can be compiled and reviewed as well;

- All the disclosures included in an OCBOA statement are supposed to be comparably as intricate as the ones included in a GAAP financial statement. They should be relevant, and the information provided in these disclosures should be clear and substantial;

- If a company has to modify an OCBOA rule, the modifications have to keep the OCBOA rule separate from a GAAP rule (and they should not result in an accounting rule that looks like a modified GAAP).

Although OCBOA accounting standards are generally accepted, it is better to stick to GAAP rules whenever possible, especially throughout the United States. This will help you ensure that your financial statements are fully compliant - but maybe even more importantly in the long run, it will help you make sure that your investors and creditors can actually read, compare, and analyze your statements at their true value, and provide you with the help you need based on an honest view of your company's financial status.

Chapter 11:

Why Your Business Needs QuickBooks

As a business owner, you understand just how important proper bookkeeping is for your business. You may have been keeping your books the traditional way – using pen and paper – but times have changed, and so have government regulations.

You may be thinking about acquiring an accounting software system for your business. You may have even considered different types of software in the market. But then the question is why should you use QuickBooks and not any other software package? Is QuickBooks really necessary for your business? What is so special about QuickBooks anyway?

Reasons for Maintaining an Accounting System

Before we look at why QuickBooks are the right solution for your business accounting needs, let's first ask why an accounting system is important.

There are two essential reasons why your business needs to maintain an accounting system. The first is government regulations. The government requires that businesses use a logical (easily understandable) accounting system that shows how much money it has made. This is meant to enable the computation of taxable income.

Now, it is understandable if you think that the government is simply a big leech trying to suck your profits in the form of ever-increasing taxes. You may even try to ignore this requirement altogether. However, this is never a good idea, and plenty a business owner has ended up on the wrong side of the law. You risk a fine or worse – jail time.

Fortunately, you are a law-abiding citizen and therefore we move on to the second reason why your business needs an accounting system. Believe it or not, but without a decent accounting system, your business will find it very difficult to succeed. You may be a great money manager, but running a successful business requires you to accurately measure and record your income and expenditure. It is the only way to determine whether your business is making profits or losses.

A good accounting system enables you to know the financial health of your business. You have to keep track of the products and services that are making you the most money, the customers that are bringing in the big bucks, and those who aren't.

Accounting and bookkeeping may seem like a tiresome and money-draining chore, but every business owner needs a good accounting system. Your success – and maybe your freedom – depends on it!

What QuickBooks Does

The truth is that QuickBooks make your life easier. How? By helping you to record all your common business transactions in a systematic manner. QuickBooks uses an interface, called a window, which enables you to fill in important information for various transactions. For example, when recording information about a check you want to pay out, all you have to do is fill in the date, amount, and the entity you want to pay. The window you see on your screen resembles an actual check. It is the same with every other financial transaction document you regularly use. An invoice window looks like an actual invoice, and all you have to do is fill in the blanks.

One of the greatest things about QuickBooks is that every financial detail captured in a particular window, from checks to invoices, is used to populate a profit and loss report that you can use to determine the financial state of your business.

QuickBooks makes your accounting process simpler and less time-consuming. Filling in data about transactions into a few windows allows you to quickly calculate whatever financial information you need. You can automatically create a balance sheet for any time period, whenever you need one. QuickBooks also helps you track client payments and inventory.

QuickBooks also has the capability to print out forms, such as invoices, containing all the information you filled in. They also come in handy when you need to do some electronic billing and banking. You can quickly email your clients an invoice, thus saving money and time. You are also able to share your bank account details with most large banks, therefore enabling you to send funds and pay suppliers electronically.

Reasons for Using QuickBooks

If you are looking for a great accounting system for your business, then QuickBooks is the best way to go. QuickBooks is the most widely used accounting software package on the globe. There are millions of businesses that are currently using QuickBooks as the foundation of their system, and its popularity is evident.

Here is why you should choose QuickBooks for your business:

QuickBooks is easy to use: What sets QuickBooks apart from its competitors is its ease of use. All you have to do is fill in information into a window that looks like your average financial form. As a businessperson, you are probably already familiar with forms like checks, invoices, purchase orders and the like. You don't need any special training or an accounting background to use this software package, unlike other accounting programs. In fact, QuickBooks has become so popular that rival accounting software systems have copied its simplicity. The only downside to QuickBooks level of simplicity is that it does not have adequate in-built control mechanisms provided by your conventional accounting system. This means that your financial information may not be as safe as it would normally be, though it has to be said that these security controls tend to make the system more complicated for the average user.

QuickBooks is affordable: Before QuickBooks, businesses relied on traditional accounting systems that were very expensive, somewhere in the range of thousands of dollars. Nowadays, there are a number of versions of QuickBooks available in the market. All you need is a few hundred dollars to get a basic QuickBooks system up and running.

QuickBooks is widely available and known everywhere: Almost every accountant you talk to knows about QuickBooks. Almost every business owner either has heard of or knows how to use QuickBooks. The average freelancer is aware of QuickBooks, even if they might have never used the software. There are even QuickBooks classes being taught in local colleges. This is a testament to the ubiquity of QuickBooks. This is unlike other accounting programs that only a few accountants or business owners may know how to use. The fact that QuickBooks is easy to use and cheap makes it well-known and widely used.

Chapter 12:

What is QuickBooks?

It is easy to find yourself overwhelmed by all the financial management responsibilities that come with running a small business. Keeping track of everything can be quite cumbersome. For this reason, most businesses are nowadays using accounting software to help in managing their business's finances.

QuickBooks is a set of accounting software solutions that are designed to help small business owners effectively and accurately organize their payroll, sales, inventory, and other accounting needs. This type of software can be used by just about anyone, as it does not require much accounting experience.

In other words, QuickBooks help you keep track of the income and expenditure of your business, generate reports and invoices, process credit card payments, and handle any other basic accounting processes.

Brief Background

The QuickBooks software package is a product developed and marketed by Intuit Inc. It is primarily targeted at small business owners, the majority of whom have no formal accounting experience. This has led to its massive popularity among small and medium-sized companies.

When QuickBooks accounting software was initially released, it did not meet the security and conventional accounting standards that the majority of professional accountants desired. However, QuickBooks has come a long way in terms of improving its features and security controls. It now has double-entry as well as full audit trail functionalities.

Intuit has also released more versions of QuickBooks accounting software, ranging from the basic package for beginners to the Pro version for more advanced users. There is also an industry-specific version that is designed for whatever business type you own. Medium-sized businesses have also been catered for by the release of a QuickBooks accounting package designed with an array of advanced features. Features of QuickBooks Software

QuickBooks now offers a number of web-based features, such as remote access, online banking, e-payment capabilities, remote payroll assistance,

Google Maps integration, and may other useful features. You can also track your employee's time, as well as import Excel spreadsheets. QuickBooks is now configured to run on both Windows OS as well Mac OS.

Factors to Consider For QuickBooks First-Timers

If you happen to be somewhat familiar with QuickBooks and understand how to use it, then this chapter is not for you. You can go ahead and skip this part. However, if you are using this accounting software for the first time, there are certain things you need to consider if you want to survive your initial interaction with QuickBooks.

1. **Keep your business and personal accounts separate**

    QuickBooks provides a really useful service by allowing you to sync your checking account with the software. Whatever transactions you perform are automatically displayed and no manual filling in of information is required. However, if you are in the habit of using money in the business account for personal use, this feature can be a problem for your business. It is recommended that you have an account for business and another one for personal use.

2. **Don't use estimates and invoices at first**

   Though the estimates and invoices features are very useful, avoid using them until you know more about QuickBooks. Why? Whenever you use these features, your accounting activity is automatically posted in QuickBooks. It is recommended that beginners create estimates and invoices on a separate program, for example, MS Word, and then manually enter that data into QuickBooks. When you have understood how QuickBooks generates these amounts, then you can go ahead and use the QuickBooks Estimates and Invoices features.

3. **Ask for help from a professional QuickBooks advisor**

   If you make a bad error and you don't know how to solve it, you should consider looking for help. Intuit has a system that enables you to find a QuickBooks Pro advisor in your local area. If you cannot afford to hire a professional, or simply don't feel like dealing with one, you can browse Intuit's Support Database for a solution.

Chapter 13:

QuickBooks Versions for Small Businesses

When QuickBooks was first released, small businesses could only use the one version that was available. Today, there are several different versions of QuickBooks that business owners can use for accounting and bookkeeping purposes. There are also some QuickBooks versions that are very specific to certain industries.

The question that needs to be asked is this – How do you know which one to choose? These different versions are priced differently and offer a variety of applications. In this chapter, you will learn the different versions of QuickBooks and how to decide which one is perfect for your business needs. Though some are well-suited for the majority of small businesses, it is still important to understand what is available to you prior to investing in a particular solution.

Which QuickBooks Version Should You Buy?

The information provided above has given you the understanding of the different versions available, their features, pros, and cons. When it comes to narrowing down which one to choose for your business, you have to ask yourself a series of questions:

Does your business use Macs?

If your business relies on Mac software, then it is best to buy QuickBooks Mac or use QuickBooks Online. Alternatively, if you have a Mac computer but want to use QuickBooks Pro or Premier, you can still do so. The only issue is that you will have to use these versions within a Windows emulator, which will increase your support costs.

Does your business handle a lot of general accounting functions?

QuickBooks Pro is considered the workhorse accounting software of all the various versions available. It can handle a large volume of the daily bookkeeping tasks that any small business deals with. It is also very user-friendly.

Do you run your business on-the-go or remotely?

If you want to be able to access your files anywhere and at any time, choose QuickBooks Online. It is perfectly suited for a company that is fast-moving and can be run from any location. There is also the option of choosing QuickBooks Pro, which now comes with a mobile data and remote access. However, this option will incur your business an extra monthly charge on top of the license fee.

Do you need a version that is specific to your industry?

If you would prefer an option that makes it easier to maneuver according to the industry your business operates in, go for QuickBooks Premier. It will provide all the features tailored for your industry, for example, increased invent controls.

Does your business need to track inventory for both raw materials and finished products?

QuickBooks Pro would normally be a good fit for most businesses, but unfortunately, it does not provide adequate inventory tracking. For a business that handles a lot of inventory of raw material as well as finished products, QuickBooks Premier would be the way to go. It has all the features necessary for such an enterprise.

QuickBooks Pro Edition

Without a doubt, this is the QuickBooks version that users love the most. Why? The reason is that QuickBooks Pro offers the most comprehensive business accounting features that any company can use, all for a reasonable fee.

If your small business is being run on the Windows platform, you should opt for either QuickBooks Pro or the more advanced QuickBooks Premier.

These are the features that QuickBooks Pro offers:

- Step-by-step tutorials
- Supports three simultaneous users
- Tracking of payments, expenses, bills, and inventory
- Tracking time and expenses related to a specific customer
- Tracking sales, sales tax, and client accounts
- Batch invoicing
- Managing payroll

- Accepting credit cards
- Creating customizable reports, invoices, and estimates

QuickBooks Enterprise

This version of QuickBooks is designed for an organization that is large enough to have a small accounting department. It seeks to cater for slightly larger businesses than the other versions and provides the organization with a bigger data set. Here are some of its additional features:

- It has a 100,000-inventory limit
- It is able to support up to 30 users at once
- It enables management of employees and fixed assets
- It can be integrated into other business systems

The license fees are not beyond the reach of an average small business owner. It might cost anything from $5000 to $10,000 annually. If your company is still small, go for the Pro or Premier version, but as it grows larger, you should consider upgrading to the Enterprise accounting software.

QuickBooks Online Edition

An online version of QuickBooks was released to suit those business professionals who wanted to access QuickBooks on–the-go. The online version is also great if you want to pay for the software whenever you need to rather than having to upgrade a desktop version. If you are a businessman or consultant who is constantly on the move, then QuickBooks Online should work well for you.

One of the best advantages of using QuickBooks Online is compatibility with all kinds of platforms. This is because the software is hosted and run on Intuit servers rather than an individual laptop, desktop, or mobile device. This makes sure that your data is secure and protected while ensuring that you make use of the latest software version. QuickBooks Online also has a set of features that are distinct from the desktop versions available. You can also retrieve your files anywhere and at any time, as long as you have access to the Internet. On the other hand, it is more expensive to use than the desktop application if you consider the charges on an annual basis.

QuickBooks Online provides the following features:

- Payroll management
- Creating invoices and estimates

- Sending estimates, reports, and invoices
- Sharing data with accountants
- Tracking sales, sales tax, payments, and inventory
- Creating more than 100 customizable accounting reports

QuickBooks Online comes in the following five versions:

1. **Online Simple Start**

   This version does not contain many of the above useful features, hence its name. It is a basic application that is primarily used by sole proprietors and small business owners who may not need the advanced features.

   It is simple to learn and use, and is a suitable long-term solution for freelancers, startups, and individual contractors. It is also available on Android, iPad, and iPhone apps, thus making it convenient for use for small business owners on the move.

   There are menu links and tabs that help you find which kind of transaction you want to engage in. Due to its simplistic design, it may not have much value for businesses that want advanced or complex transactions. Online Simple Start comes with the following features:

- Creation and customization of invoices
- Tracking and reporting sales, taxes, and expenses
- Customization of business reports, for example, profit and loss, sales, and balance sheets
- Preparation of estimates
- Storage of client contacts
- Electronic payment of bills

The purpose of creating this version is to get small businesses to use the service for a fee as they test the waters. Once you realize that this version is inadequate for your business needs, you are expected to upgrade to a more useful version – of course at an extra cost.

2. Online Essentials

This version is slightly better than Online Simple Start, but it is still considered a basic accounting service. However, Essentials allows you to run your small business using the normal bookkeeping features. Most of the features that a normal business requires are still lacking, though. Online Essentials does not offer you features like billing by customer, budgeting and planning, inventory tracking, class tracking, tracking multiple locations, or creating purchase orders.

3. *Online Essentials with Payroll*
   This is a similar version to the one above. The only difference is that it offers your business an online payroll service.

4. **Online Plus**

   This online version of QuickBooks contains all the features that Essentials does not. If you decide to use QuickBooks over the Internet, then this is the version you need to go for. The majority of small business owners who opt for this version seem to be satisfied with what it has to offer. Online Plus provides the accounting requirements that any small business would need on a regular basis. In case your business has more complicated bookkeeping requirements, it is recommended that you get yourself a desktop software solution.

5. **Online Plus with Payroll**

   This is a similar version to the one above. The only difference is that it offers your business a payroll service.

QuickBooks for Mac

This version of QuickBooks is well-suited for a company whose computers all run on Mac. The Mac version of QuickBooks comes in a software package that is quite different from all the other versions, which use the Windows operating system.

QuickBooks Mac is designed to run on an interface that is specific for a Mac framework. This means that accessing the diverse sections and modules requires a user who is familiar with a Mac system. Though the initial versions of QuickBooks Mac were a bit unfriendly for users, the recent versions have greatly improved user experience and feel more like Mac applications.

QuickBooks for Mac has the following features:

- When it's set up the right way, it can be fun and easy to use, especially when performing online banking.

- It allows you to share your records and files with users running on a Windows system.

- It enables the user to design nice invoices that can be emailed together with a link that customers simply click to speed up cash payments.

- The accounting software also uses an online payroll that is able to sync data, thus negating the need for entering complex paychecks.

- It has a limited job costing functionality.

QuickBooks for Mac tends to develop bugs here and there, though it usually works well. The challenge with this software is in setting it up properly. There are also very few apps that are compatible with it, and collaboration with your bookkeeper is not easy at all. If you have the option of choosing between QuickBooks for Mac and online accounting software, go for the online version.

QuickBooks Premier

This particular version is designed to fit whatever industry your business operates in. You are required to choose and buy the version that will suit your specific industry, for example, general business, retail, wholesale, manufacturing, contractors, professional services, or non-profit.

QuickBooks Pro offers a customization feature that the other versions do not, and its interface changes to display a language that is specific to your industry. For example, if you work in a non-profit organization, "customers" are displayed as "donors." Even the way reports are provided is customized to suit the industry your business operates in.

QuickBooks Premier provides users with additional features to what the Pro version has, such as:

- Reporting that is specific to your industry
- Tracking your costs for inventory and finished products
- Creating track-back and sales orders
- Forecasting of sales and expenses
- Business planning tools
- Supports five simultaneous users

Chapter 14:

QuickBooks Online

Solid accounting is the number one support system in any business and QuickBooks is known as the best accounting system that is suitable for any small business. With the software, you can easily organize your sales through a good track of your expenses, organization of your timesheets, preparing of invoices and sales slips. The software will also help you keep a good track of your tax information. QuickBooks are available as QuickBooks desktop and QuickBooks online and both of them are really good. The choice that you make is mainly determined by the kind of business you are running.

QuickBooks online

QuickBooks online is the kind of program that is best suited for a business person that is always on the go therefore he can outsource a bookkeeper or an accountant. This version of QuickBooks comes with one great feature which is the cloud feature. This is the version that will enable a business person to perform customer billing automatically as well as email reports. With this version, you can keep your financial records accurately as well as get enough time to go out there to ensure that your customers are getting the information that they need on time. It is therefore a very flexible program for a business person.

This is the much-preferred version for many business people because it gives you access to the basic features of an accountant.

The cost of QuickBooks online is much lower than the QuickBooks desktop. You get to enjoy using it for free for an entire month before you can invest in the program. This is what makes it the best program for those business people that are starting up.

The cloud benefits of QuickBooks online

Buying, building and maintaining a functional IT structure is a requirement in business these days but with the increasing prices, small businesses are not able to achieve their desires because of financial limitations. The cloud gives businesses of all kinds and sizes a great alternative in that businesses can now subscribe to shared services online. The benefits of this are so many, for instance you do not have to pay for the services fully since there are several other businesses that are accessing the same services. All you need is to be able to access QuickBooks online. Some of the benefits that business people get to enjoy from this are:

1. Time savings: time is an important element in any business. Saving time might result to better results in a business since more time is sent on things that matter more in the business for the realization of better results. Cloud computing is one way through which a business can save a considerable amount of time. This is because technology and data are always available and you can count on them. One thing business people should know about is that with cloud computing, you will not have to manage your software and you will also not have to go back and forth to visit your clients or even to spend plenty of time on data entry. This is what will save you ample time as well as your business and also your clients

2. Cloud computing gives you anytime, anywhere access: the functionality of cloud is accessible to you anywhere you will be at any given time. You can access your work at any time of day or night, from wherever you might be across the globe. You always get an always-on connection to your client's data; therefore, you can still serve your clients from wherever you might be. You also do not have to deal with time zone restrictions whenever you are filing your tax

returns. This means that you are free to do so much from anywhere, anytime, for instance:

- Adding and editing employees, customers or vendors

- Viewing reports pertaining to balance sheet and profit & loss

- Creating and emailing invoices

- Viewing balances from your Bank account and credit card

- Accessing the lists of your vendors, customers, and employee

- Access of information pertaining to your debtors and creditors

3. Cloud computing makes it easy for you to work with your clients: this is one program that will intensify the bond you have with your clients, without any costs. If you have clients who want to be involved in any business operation, you will find this program really helpful. Your clients can see what work is in progress, how much has been accomplished and what still needs to be done. This is what keeps an open communication between your clients and the business.

4. It is easy to afford. With cloud computing, you can be sure that you will afford all the benefits

that it comes with. To start with, there are no license fees and this means that the initial costs are already taken care of. Generally speaking, you will incur fewer costs, which is good for business.

This is what you get from QuickBooks online

1. Automated customer billing instead of doing it manually which can be inaccurate and time consuming.

2. An automated email report which saves so much time and also provides accurate information for your clients.

3. So many people can use the program at a go.

4. It provides an activity log which enables everyone to track down what they have done so far. You can also see what your employers are doing at any given time.

5. It gives users a simultaneous access to data. You do not need to wait for one to work on a document for you to use it, which costs a business so much time.

QuickBooks desktop

This program comes with a lot of customized features which many businesses will need. It is good in inventory tracking, budgeting and time tracking. This is the program that will help you determine the area where you are spending so much money in a business in order to cut down on the expenditure to maximize on the income. Many business people use this version of QuickBooks as an investment for the benefits it offers to the business.

Chapter 15:

QuickBooks for Inventory

Businesses which deal with items for sale, whether small or large, needs to keep track of their inventory. This is what makes it easy for you to avail what your customers need at any given time without fail. With proper inventory, serving your customers effectively and on time all the time is made easy and this is what gains your business a good reputation. Besides, you are able to keep a good track record of what you have sold and what you still have in stock, which is important in balancing of accounts and helping you with payment of taxes. With such records, you will easily know when to place more order for more goods so that you will not run out of stock, which can inconvenience your clients. This can be hard to do if you are doing it manually but with QuickBooks, it can be done in no time and more accurately.

Setting up QuickBooks inventory

QuickBooks inventory is usually more involved and it can be harder when compared to other areas in the business. This is maybe because inventory affects all the other areas in a business, starting with sales, purchasing, production, accounting, shipping among others. This is the entry that shows workflow processes in a business, because the transaction that one person handles in a given department will result to another transaction in the same or different department.

Another reason why this is the most important entry is because so many lists come into play once inventory is affected and the entire database is affected in the end. What this means is that once a transaction has been executed, vendor and customer information in the database is touched. Every item in the inventory has so many attributes, for instance the average cost, the selling price, buying price, unit of measure among so many others. Again, the item has to go through several transactional processes. If an item is being bought for instance, it will have to go through the purchase orders, item receipts, and vendor bills among others. If it is being sold, there are such transaction processes like sales orders, estimates, packing lists, pick tickets, invoices among others. In short, transactions under inventory are connected to so many other entries that are affected once a single transaction is made, that is why this is the most complex thing you will handle with QuickBooks.

Many people make the mistake of rushing through inventory just as they would do when handling a simple data entry then they realize the mistake they have made when it is already too late. You need to adopt a systematic approach in order to set up your inventory in an accurate manner:

Prepare your lists

Your inventory is not just about the list of items; there are other lists that you have to prepare for instance the chart of accounts, the units of measure, the vendor lists, the location and tracking lists among others. Your lists will form the foundation for the inventory. The good thing about using QuickBooks here is that all the items will be connected to the financial accounts; therefore you will not have to worry so much about the accounting bit because it is already taken care of. What you do is that you start with the accounting part, and then connect all the items you will enter in the inventory to the account one at a time. You will not have to go back to balance your accounts when this is done the right way.

First of all let us consider the main accounts in the Chart of Accounts, which affect any items in the inventory:

- An Inventory Asset account that is on the Balance Sheet

- An Income account that is on the Profit & Loss Statement or income statement

- A Cost of Goods Sold account which is also on the Profit & Loss Statement.

You have to choose which of these three accounts you will attach to your items; the ones which will help you make the best reports and accurate financial results. To do this, turn on the inventory function in QuickBooks by the administrator, go to Edit, then Preferences, Items and Inventory, Company Preferences tab then click to activate Inventory and purchase orders. When this is done, your software will automatically create an Inventory Asset account as the other asset type of account, which cannot be changed again.

You might need to create other Inventor Asset accounts depending on how the company plans to trail the value of their inventory. If for instance you are a manufacturing company that needs to track the work-in-progress, you might need several of these accounts but for a distributor, one account will be enough.

Pay attention to the Inventory valuation summary report, which lists down everything in the inventory and all the items in the stock lists. This is the report which shows balances in the inventory asset accounts. The total in this report and the totals in the inventory asset account can be used as a checks and balances to show that you are recording your items properly; therefore, both of them should always match.

The next bit you should take care of is the creation of a **Sales or Income account**. This is the second most important account type in the Charts of Accounts. A mistake that is common with many QuickBooks beginners is that they create so many income accounts probably for every product that they deal with. These many accounts will be hard to manage in the end and you will be spending so much time on it, more than you should. An easier way out is to have maybe two or three accounts for your product lines. If you want to track down profitability for instance, you can easily do this through reports=Jobs, Time and Mileage=Item Profitability Report. It is important to know that items in your business will all get connected to one account, therefore if you are selling to different people and you want to track down your sales separately, it is easier to use classes in QuickBooks than to create different accounts for them.

The third most important account under Charts of Accounts is the **Cost of Goods Sold account**. This account is automatically created once you turn on the inventory function in QuickBooks. With this account too, there might be need for more than one account, although it is not really necessary unless there is a good reason for it. It is important to know that every item you will have in your inventory will only connect to one of these accounts therefore only create an additional account if you have a need for additional reports.

After the accounts have been created, you can now work on the **Units of Measure**. This is the trickiest lists under inventory in QuickBooks. This list will determine the kind of goods you will receive, the kind of stock you will keep and also the kinds of goods you will be selling. You will have to decide if you will be dealing with multiple units of measure or just a single unit, which is bought and sold on the same unit. This function will be turned on under the Preferences=Items and Inventory. Before you set your Units of Measure list, consider these issues:

- The base unit of items- this will be the smallest unit of items that have been received, stacked or sold. This is the unit that will be used to determine the unit which will be used in purchases and sales, because these units come as multiples of the base unit. This way, you will not have to deal with fractions or another unit.

- The base unit will be the only one that will reflect in QuickBooks' Inventory Stock Status report. You will not get any report pertaining to multiple units in your stocks.

- Different types of units of measure can be set up for instance weight, volume etc. but ensure that the quantities of these units will not change depending on the product that has been affected.

The **vendor list** is another important list you will have to consider before you start recording items in your inventory. You can have this list compiled then import it into the QuickBooks file like many business people do. Ensure that you have an up-to-date vendor list so as to save time since you will not have to specify the vendor later on.

If you are using an advanced inventory function, you will have two more lists to prepare: location list and also serial or lot number tracking list. You can prepare the location ahead of time, and then add it to the inventory function through the Lists dropdown menu.

Types of items in the items list

Now that you have all the lists prepared, you can now proceed to the list of items. Here are the basic types of items that you will have under this list:

1. Services: under this category, you will record the labor that is purchased from a vendor or labor that has been included in an invoice for a customer. If it is just used for your customers, it will only need to connect to an income account.

2. The inventory: this will have a list of raw materials or items that are needed for resale and this part will help in case you want to trail the quantity that is in stock. The value of items in this list will be under inventory asset account until they are sold, because this is the time their cost will be recognized through their invoice.

3. Non-inventory parts: these are items that are only expensed at the time of purchase. With these items, the manager does not really know how many they are at any given time. These items will appear in the purchase and sale documents.

4. Inventory assemblies: this is a list of items that are as a result of assembling of components or items that have been produced through raw materials processing/manufacturing. Again, the value of items here will be stored in the inventory asset account until the items are sold, which is when their costs will be recognized through the invoice.

5. Group Items: these are items in components that are sold as just one item. Once they are sold, that is the time QuickBooks will reduce the

quantity of their components. These items are usually not kept in stock therefore their quantities are not usually tracked.

6. The other charge: these may not be actual inventory items but they are related to inventory although it is hard to specify a unit of measure on them. These are for instance handling charges.

7. there are so many other items types you might want to include for instance discounts, sales tax, payments among other although they do not affect inventory directly.

It is important to determine the inventory type where your items will fall into first, and then you can easily enter them in those categories. The inventories list and the assemblies for instance will connect to the three accounts I mentioned above while services, other charge and non-inventory items can use the purchasing account, the sales account or both of them, depending on whether the items has been sold or bought or it has been bought for resale. Group item on the other hand will not be connected to any of these accounts because their existence is after a certain component has been removed.

Chapter 16:

14 Tips and Tricks

Any business finance software is supposed to make accounting much easier and more reliable and QuickBooks is very easy to use software. However, there is always a way that you can make things easier even when you are using this software. This will make achieving your desired results easier than you previously thought. If you have already started QuickBooks, here are some tips and tricks that can help you achieve more from QuickBooks:

1. Use of keyboard shortcuts: most if not all windows-based applications come with some shortcuts that can make working easy for you and QuickBooks is not exceptional. There are several shortcuts that you can always employ in order to work faster and to enjoy your accounting, some of these are:

    - Ctrl-I to create an invoice

    - Ctrl-N to open a new item like a check, invoice, a bill

- Ctrl-F to find a transaction

- Ctrl-W to write a new check

- Ctrl-E to edit a transaction that has been selected in the register

- Ctrl-J to open customer support center

- Ctrl-M to memorize a certain transaction or report

2. Customizing the icon bar to suit your needs: a new QuickBooks program will come with a default icons bar at the top of the screen. This bar can be customized in order to suit your preference and needs. This can be done by removing, adding or even modifying some icons to ensure that they fit just what you need to work with. Removing an item form the icons bar for instance can be achieved by clicking on it and hitting the delete button. To add an icon on the other hand, you will click on the field where you want to add the icon, click on item, hit the add button then select the icons that you want to add from the drop down menu. You can also change the way icons appear on the icon bar or even add separators, just what you want for your icons bar.

3. Right click on menus anywhere in the program: doing this will be much easier than going for the icons and menus on the tool bar. If you want to

do something on the menu, you can right click on it and do whatever needs to be done. If for instance you want to make changes on a certain entry in the Chart of counts, you can right click on it and then you will be able to delete it, edit it, customize it or anything that you prefer. This makes changing anything much easier and faster.

4. Use of the Quick Math calculator: QuickBooks comes with its own calculator. To access it, you click on 'edit' then 'use calculator'. However, the Quick Math calculator will be much easier and better to use. To use it, click on the field where you want to make a calculation, click on the = sign to get a mini-tape. Type in the numbers that will be used in the calculation followed by the sign that you want to use in the calculation. If you want to clear out an entry, click once on C but to clear everything from the tape, you will have to click on C twice. To cancel the entry calculation, click on Esc

5. Use of Classes to track profit and loss better: elements of a business are categorized in classes in QuickBooks. Every entry that you enter will be categorized under a certain class. Class reports are important because they are the ones that determine if the business is getting into a loss or making profits. Whenever you are working with your reference, you have to make sure that classes are turned on. This way, every transaction that you enter will be categorized

under a certain class. With this, you should be able to get a class report of every element in your business to know how well or ad you are doing.

6. Backing your data up to the cloud: the program will come with a wizard that will take you through the process of backing up your data up to the cloud. This ensures that your data will be absolutely safe and that it can be accessible from any computer anywhere, anytime. This comes at a small cost though, but the benefits you get here are more than what you pay for them.

7. Use of edit/preferences feature: a QuickBooks program will come with a set up wizard that will help you set up the groundwork for your business. You do not have to stick to this wizard though because it is not comprehensive. You can edit to the kind of setup that you want for your business, one that suits your business needs. To do this, you will have to click on the edit/preferences button to make more decisions, which are not available in the setup wizard. Some of the decisions that you can make here are for instance the kind of default accounts you will be using for writing checks and paying bills, the default annual interest rate you will be using for your business, if you want to create estimates or not, whether or not you want to use payroll, the kinds of reminders you will be using among others.

8. If you are using more than one checking account in your business, you can always change the background color of your accounts in order to easily identify one account from the other/others. To do this, open the register for any of the checking accounts whose background color you want to change, click on the edit menu then select 'change account color'. This will make it easy for you to identify one account from the others.

9. Plan for the Major Expenses

There are times when a big expense is going to come up. If you don't plan for these issues, you will put yourself in trouble with money, miss out on some big opportunities, or have to go out with something. When you plan for these major expenses, and they are going to show up at some point, you will either have to miss out on a business opportunity that is important to you, or you may have to scramble for a loan from the bank if you have to pay. For example, if your computer system crashes and you need to pay for some IT to come in, it is much better to have this money on hand rather than scrambling to get a loan and get it fixed in time.

There are several things that you can do when this happens. First, put some big events, like a computer upgrade that is needed, on the calendar a year in advance. If you can, write this down every year for the next three to five years. You can also acknowledge on the calendar some of the seasonal ups and downs the business has and make sure that you are putting enough money aside to make it through these leaner months as well.

Often the costly things that you need to fix are going to show up in the slower months for your company. Do you really want to get caught in the trap of taking out money during the busy periods, just to find out that you are short on money for major repairs in some of the slower months?

10. Set Money for Your Taxes

If you are past the first year of business, or you are a sole proprietorship who owed the IRS $1,000 or more for a year, then you need to file quarterly tax returns. If you fail to do this, then the IRS could levy interest and penalties for not filing these on time.

The best thing to do is to systematically put some of the money aside during the year that you can use to pay your taxes. Then, on the calendar, you will note the deadlines for the taxes, along with any preparation time if it is needed. This ensures that you are actually able to make the tax payments to the IRS on time when they are due.

One thing that can be especially problematic for your business is payroll taxes. There are times when some entrepreneurs, who aren't taking care of their finances properly, will be crash-crunched and end up in a down cycle. They will dip into the employee withholdings, the money that was earmarked to be sent to the IRS.

If you start messing with these payroll taxes, you are going to end up with a twofold problem. First, you haven't paid the taxes that are due for the employees, and you have taken money that the IRS sees as belonging to the employees. The IRS is not going to be very happy about this situation, and you will end up in a lot of trouble. Set aside some money to help you pay your quarterly taxes.

11. Track All the Expenses

You want to keep accurate records of all the expenses and transactions that come up with your business. Tracking these not only gives you a good idea on how the finances of the business are doing, but it can help you with tax season. If you don't keep good track of the expenses that you take on during the year, you might miss some tax write-offs or have to give up on a few because you just don't have the right information.

Having the right bookkeeping methods in place, and keeping all the receipts of your business along the way, can help you out here. You should either have everything added and uploaded to your online bookkeeping software or have another system of accounting that you can work with to help keep everything organized. This will go a long way in helping you see results.

This means that you should keep track of everything that you do with your business and every expense that you take for the business. This includes any events that take cash, any coffee dates, lunches, and business trips, should be kept track of. This habit is going to go a long way toward substantiating those items for your tax records in case you are audited. These records make sure that you are safe in case the IRS wants to look at your records and can make it easier to know what tax deductions you get in the first place.

12. Record the Deposits Correctly

The reason that this one is so important is that it makes it less likely that you are going to pay taxes on money that isn't income. You never want to pay more taxes than you need to, especially when it comes to paying it on money that isn't your income.

The best thing here is to take up a system that will keep all the financial activities of your business straight, whether it is a notebook that you use on a regular basis, the help of an Excel spreadsheet, or some software that can record all your financial information.

Being a business owner, you need to make a wide variety of deposits into your bank account throughout a fiscal year, including deposits about revenue from any sales, cash infusions from the personal savings, or loans. The trouble here is that when the year ends, you (or a bookkeeping you decide to work with), might go through this information and then record some of the deposits as income when they aren't your income. And when this happens, you could end up paying taxes on more money than what you actually made that year.

13. The Best Bookkeeping Tips for Your Business

As a new entrepreneur, you have a lot of financial details that you have to keep track of to help the business run efficiently. Doing this well has a lot of advantages. It can help you to make sure that you are making profits and understand exactly where your money is going each month. It helps you to be prepared for tax season at the end of the year. And it can ensure that you are paying your employees properly and that your business is growing the way that you want.

Getting started with bookkeeping may seem a bit confusing when you first get started. There are many different forms that you need to pay attention to, and this can be scary for a lot of beginners who have never experienced these before. Let's look at some of the best bookkeeping tips that you can follow to help your business stay financially secure.

14. Keep a Tab on the Invoices That You Have

You will quickly find in your business that any late bills or unpaid bills are going to cut into the cash flow that you have. When people are not paying the invoice that they owe to you, and you had to pay for employees to do the work and materials, this can really end up putting you behind. You had to pay for everything upfront, and now you have to make due and keep getting things paid upfront for other customers, without having that money from the original customers.

You have to always keep track of the invoices that you have to make sure they are all paid on time. It is important to designate someone in your company to keep track of your billing. Then put a process in place so that you can make phone calls, send out a second invoice, and levying penalties, such as extra fees at a certain deadline.

When it comes to the invoices that you have, you want to make sure that you have a plan in the event one of your customers doesn't pay their bill to you yet, since this can influence the cash flow so much. Come up with a plan of what you will need to do if the customer is thirty, sixty, or ninety days late on an invoice that you sent them.

Don't fall into the trap of thinking that once you sent out an invoice to a customer, that your billing is taken care of. Every late payment is basically an interest-free loan, and it is going to seriously harm the cash flow of your business. You want to keep sending out invoices and have a good plan in place to ensure that you are getting the message out to your customer and that they will pay for the product or service.

Chapter 17:

Mistakes to Avoid

The way that you keep your company's files talks a lot about the kind of person you are and the kind of business that you are running. So many business people strive to keep their business record in good order but most of them do not success and the funny bit is that most of the mistakes that they make are similar. Sometimes making such mistakes happens even when you are very careful that is why it is important to know some of this common mistake so that you will be careful with in order to leave all your financial statements accurate and easy to interpret.

1. Failing to reconcile your accounts: accounts reconciliation is very important because the integrity of any account is dependent on reconciliation. Reconciliations ensure that what you have in all your accounts is correct, that is why it is a very important part of the process. Do not just concentrate on your checking and savings accounts but also on liabilities, which include loans and taxes. Also ensure that you check on asset accounts as well, since all the accounts are

important in any business. This is the only way you will be sure that everything in your register is accurate.

2. Skipping credit card accounts: many business people will not include their credit card into the QuickBooks, which is a regrettable mistake. This issue of creating an expense account every time you credit your credit card or making it an item in the check window is not good. You need to have an account for that, just like a checking account so that you will keep your records well and easy to follow through. Once you make a payment into the credit card, it should be a transfer of money to the credit card and nothing else.

3. Deleting transactions: there is no single transaction in QuickBooks that work independently; all of them are connected to other transactions, therefore any change that you will make on one transaction will affect so many others. If you delete one entry for instance, you will change the entire data. You need to check with your accountant first before deleting any transaction to ensure that it is not affecting many entries in your system.

4. Failing to review the balance sheet: reviewing your balance sheet will help you understand the financial health of your business. Since the balance sheet reflects all the accounts you have in your business. It is easy to know how well you are doing, or even how bad things are. Your

statements from the accounts should all match; otherwise you should know that there is a major issue in your business. This is the only way you can make sound decisions pertaining to your business in order to better its performance.

5. Not using your purchase order system: this is a very important tool but not many people get to enjoy its usefulness. What you do is to make sure that you create a purchase order very time you make an order from a vendor. You always have to ensure that you are receiving your orders against that PO. Do not keep such records for over a year though so as not to keep records that are no longer useful in your system.

6. Use of multiple accounts and subaccounts: this is what creates a messy chart of accounts and it is a mistake that many bookkeepers make because they think that it will help them understand the reports better. However, this will take so much of your time and your reports can be confusing for another person who will be reading them. You do not need so many subaccounts when you can group some of these items together into one account. Instead of having separate accounts for pen and papers for instance, you can have a stationary account for them all. Keep your accounts as simple as possible.

7. A disorderly items list: every product that you sell will be listed as items in QuickBooks. Sometimes people just record and inventory anywhere and

they do not remember to keep the records updated. You need to clean this up because it will mess up your entire records. In order to achieve a clean items list, deactivate all the items that you are no longer selling. All the items should fall under inventory and non-inventory categories. Also, ensure that the costs for each items is up to date. You should also double check the items that are in stock at all times.

8. Use of incorrect report settings: report settings are very important; hence you have to ensure that you are using them in their correct settings. This way, you will get the proper report when you need it. Accrual reports for instance should give you information pertaining to the overall performance of your business. Cash reports on the other hand should show you how cash is flowing in and out of the business.

Chapter 18:

Definitions of Bookkeeping terms

Bookkeeping

Bookkeeping is the process of recording business transactions. Bookkeeping establishes the foundation for accounting.

Accounting

Accounting is the process of preparing financial statements by summarizing the business transactions recorded through bookkeeping. Accounting also includes analyzing and reporting financial information in a manner that facilitates business decision making.

Revenues

Revenues are all monies earned by a business in any given period of time. Revenues can be derived from sales of goods, sales of services, interest, and any miscellaneous sources.

However, capital deposits are not revenues. Also, monies from loans are not to be considered as revenues either.

Expenses

Expenses are all monies spent by a business. Operating expenses are expenses directly related to the normal operation of a business, which include rents, salaries, supplies, etc. Operating expenses tend to be recurring.

Nonoperation expenses are expenses not related to the normal operation of a business. As such, no operating expenses are usually not recurring. One example of no operating expenses would be the settlement cost of a lawsuit.

Profits

After ascertaining the total amount of revenues and the total amount of expenses, **profit** (1) can be calculated via a profit equation as follows:

Profit = Revenues - Expenses

The main goal of many businesses is to increase profits. It is clear from the profit equation that profit can be increased by increasing revenues and/or reducing expenses.

Deductible Expenses

Under the Internal Revenue Code, certain business expenses (both operating and no operating expenses) are considered as tax **deductible expenses**. In order to minimize income tax payments, a business owner should become familiar with the tax treatment of various deductible expenses.

Many business expenses are deductible in their entirety in the fiscal year (2) in which they are incurred, and some examples of such business expenses are as follows:

Advertising parking fees

Bad debts postage

Bank charges printing

Commission's professional services

Contract services profit-sharing plans

Donations rent

Dues repairs

Educational fees/materialssalaries

Food and entertainmentsubscriptions

Insurance taxes

Legal fees telephone

License fees tools

Loan interest uniforms

Office equipment utility bills

Office suppliesvehicle expenses

Depreciable Assets

Instead of the deductible in their entirety in the year in which they are incurred, the expenses on certain business assets, such as business properties, production machinery, office furniture, vehicles, etc., need to be deducted over multiple years. This group of assets is known as **depreciable assets**. The method for deducting the costs of depreciable assets over multiple years is known as **depreciation**.

Section 179 Deduction

Under § 179 of the Internal Revenue Code, when a depreciable asset is qualified as a **qualifying property**, a business is allowed to treat all or part of the cost of the depreciable asset as an expense completely deductible in the year in which it is incurred, instead of over multiple years.

Assets, Liabilities, and Equity

The financial condition of a business can be expressed by the relationship of **assets** to **liabilities** and **owner's equity**.

Assets are all properties owned by a business. Assets include current assets and long-term assets. Current assets are items that can be converted into cash within one year or less, such as cash-in-bank and account receivable. Long-term assets are any assets that are not considered as current assets, such as property and equipment.

Liabilities are all debts the business currently has outstanding to creditors. Liabilities include current liabilities and long-term liabilities. Current liabilities are debts that need to be paid off within one year or less, such as account payable. Long-term liabilities are any liabilities that are not considered as current liabilities.

Owner's equity is the interest of an owner in the business. Owner's equity may include capital and retained earnings.

Accounting Equation

Assets, liabilities and owner's equity are related to each other via a fundamental equation known as the **accounting equation**. The accounting equation states that, without exceptions, the following relationship must always be true:

Assets = Liabilities + Owner's Equity

According to the accounting equation, a business is assumed to possess its assets subject to the rights of its creditors and owners.

For example, when a business owns assets of $200,000, owes creditors $120,000, and owes the business owner $80,000, the accounting equation looks like this:

200,000 = 120,000 + 80,000

AssetsLiabilities Owner's Equity

After a period of time, when the business pays off $15,000 of the debt, the liabilities are reduced by $15,000. If the assets are not changed, the owner's equity is increased by $15,000, and the accounting equation becomes this:

200,000 = 105,000 + 95,000

AssetsLiabilities Owner's Equity

Transaction

A **transaction** is any business event that alters the amount of assets, liabilities, and/or owner's equity.

Journalizing

Every transaction must be recorded as an entry in a journal in chronological order, and the process is called **journalizing**.

Conclusion

This book has given you the tools to better understand not only your bookkeeper but your business as well. These are all areas that you, as a business owner, need to know and understand.

Each area that we have covered has a purpose. When you work hand-in-hand with your bookkeeper, you will see the light at the end of the tunnel.

I mentioned in the beginning, "It is not the business owner that runs the business. It is the business owner teamed up with the bookkeeper that truly runs the business."

I want to take a minute to break down that statement. As the business owner, you have the power to make the decisions that will move your business forward. Your business will succeed or fail based on your decisions.

Your bookkeeper is the gatekeeper. They hold power over the financial health of your business. With their mighty power, you can have all the financial statements you need when you need them. They can also ensure that all the transactions are correct.

As a team, you are unstoppable. Your bookkeeper can ensure you have what is needed to move your business in the right direction. They can also help guide you in making the right decisions. With the proper analysis and ratios, you can predict the future if the trend is steady.

Now I have empowered you to be on the same level as your bookkeeper and accountant.

If you have not started your business yet but you are thinking about it and currently doing the research for your business, then this is a great place to start.

With the knowledge that you have learned, you will also be better prepared to add your financials to your business plan and pitch deck.

Best of luck to all your endeavors. I look forward to seeing your business up and running and hearing about the great success you will be having.

www.ingramcontent.com/pod-product-compliance
Lightning Source LLC
Chambersburg PA
CBHW021816170526
45157CB00007B/2611